DEFYING GRAVITY

DEFYING GRAVITY

The Making of Newton

Doug Menuez	Photography
Markos Kounalakis	Text
Paul Saffo	Introduction

BEYOND WORDS PUBLISHING, INC.

13950 NW Pumpkin Ridge Road.

Hillsboro, Oregon 97124

503-647-5109

Text copyright © 1993 by Beyond Words Publishing, Inc.

Photography copyright © 1993 by Doug Menuez

Distributed to the book trade by Publishers Group West

Printed in the United States of America

This book is printed on recycled paper.

DESIGN: Principia Graphica

PRINTING: Dynagraphics

BINDING: Lincoln & Allen

ELECTRONIC PREPRESS: Exact Imaging

EDITOR: Julie Livingston

PICTURE EDITOR: Michele McNally

All rights reserved. No part of this book may be reproduced or transmitted in any form or by any means, electronic or mechanical, including photocopying, recording, or by any information storage and retrieval system, without the written permission of the Publisher, except where permitted by law.

Beyond Words Publishing Inc. corporate mission:

INSPIRE TO INTEGRITY

Library of Congress Cataloging-in-Publication Data

Menuez, Doug.

  Defying gravity : the making of Newton / Doug Menuez, photography; Markos Kounalakis, text.

    p. cm.

  ISBN 0-941831-94-9 : $29.95

1. Apple Computer, Inc. 2. Computer software industry—United States—Case studies. I. Menuez, Doug. II. Title.

HD9696.C64A866 1993   93-28081

338.7'61004'0973—dc20   CIP

Hip info-gizmo, outlandish vision and the catalyst for a chain reaction that will atom-smash an aging personal-computer order into oblivion—Newton is all three, and that is only part of the story. As much a portent of things to come as a product in its own right, it has burst onto the computing scene like a comet in the dawn sky. It is the first tangible proof of a revolution in the making, a device whose mere announcement created an entire new hardware market.

This is a revolution for the rest of us, for everyone who finds personal computers irrelevant annoyances, useless encumbrances in daily life. The Newton MessagePad is the first in a coming constellation of ultra-portable information devices that will deliver not just ease of use, but usefulness to tasks far beyond spreadsheets and word-processing arcana. By decade's end, these new tools will mature into ubiquitous and unobtrusive assistants for ordinary people with real, everyday needs. The computers of the 1980s were personal, but Newton and its familiars will be intimate.

Against the backdrop of this larger revolution, it is clear that Newton at once defies and submits to the twin gravitational forces of habit and innovation. It will not be long before Newton will seem the obvious consequence of an inevitable convergence of emerging technologies and evolving user needs. Yet the intimacy that defines Newton is also an act of innovative defiance, for its corporate parent is above all a personal-computer company. Apple's future depends on entry into this brave new world of information appliances, but from the moment of Newton's conception, change-loathing corporate antibodies within the company threatened to extinguish the infant machine. As Newton's

builders soon discovered, bringing Newton to market was comparable to breaking free from the gravitational pull of the sun.

The same battles are being waged in companies throughout the computer and consumer electronics industries as other teams work to turn their visions into product realities. The stake is far larger than dominance of an emerging market, for we stand at a critical moment in American business history, where the winners will determine the shape of the high-technology landscape as we enter the next century.

Defying Gravity thus is much more than a mere record of the birth of a new machine. Apple granted unprecedented, editorially independent access to Doug Menuez and Markos Kounalakis, allowing them to shadow Newton and its makers on a manic, globe-trotting race fraught with wild reverses and uncertainty. Add in Menuez' skills as an accomplished and edge-surfing photojournalist, and Kounalakis' ability to tease the essence from present-tense chaos, and the result is a record of innovation unparalleled in the history of Silicon Valley.

We are fortunate that one story is now preserved in images and text as it unfolded, without the palliative gloss of corporate revisionists. This is a tale of innovation as it actually happened, delivered by authors who properly concluded that Newton was setting in motion forces that ultimately could touch and change all of our lives.

Above all, this is a story of people, for Newton represents the incarnation of the hopes and visions of its makers who, against all odds, elected to build their brainchild inside Apple. Silicon Valley is steeped in the mythology of entrepreneurship. It is a place where engineers hone their skills while employed by corporate giants, saving their best ideas for the day when they can start companies of their own. Newton's creators resisted the myth, becoming instead *intrapreneurs*, innovators within Apple encouraged by visionary CEO John Sculley, pursuing their heretical vision with single-minded determination. If Newton succeeds, their organizational innovation could become a new norm in Valley mythology, shaping team after team to come.

"If Newton succeeds"—that is indeed the question at the fore as this book goes to press, for Newton's success is far from a sure thing. It is a new machine in an unknown market, where the smallest weakness could spell disaster. Newton's path ahead is not unlike that of a comet picking its way through the solar system, racing toward a slingshot rendezvous around the sun.

Whatever happens, the first Newton is unlikely to be in our lives longer than a cometary visitor might hover in the skies above us. MessagePad is but the first in a family of products incorporating the Newton technology, many of which are already taking shape behind closed doors at Apple and elsewhere. If MessagePad succeeds among early adopters—individuals eager to take a risk on intriguing novelties—these future Newtons will follow one another to the market even more rapidly than successive versions of the Macintosh, for this computer revolution will unfold at the breakneck pace of consumer electronics.

As these words are written, the MessagePad's August debut lies some weeks in the future. The possibility of failure has to be on the minds of its creators—it would be fate-tempting hubris for them to ignore the bleak history of consumer electronics innovation. This history tells us that new information tools such as Newton and its competitors are more likely to fail than not, and the most its inventors can hope for is that it will fail in interesting ways that will inform the design of its second- and third-generation progeny.

But Newton has already defied corporate innovation-crushing gravity, so I suspect that its introduction will confound the naysayers and even surprise the enthusiasts. MessagePad looks like a cliff-hanger, but I believe that Newton's short-term success could match that of the original Macintosh. Newton's long-term prospects are less certain, though if failure comes, it is more likely to be the consequence of a loss of nerve by executives elsewhere at Apple than the fault of the Newton team. This is a revolution that will package computing devices in consumer electronics skins in order to make them useful. The line between brilliant irresistibility and absurd irrelevance is thin indeed—and impossible to anticipate. An uncountable number of new gizmos are about to burst on consumers, and most will prove to be information Hula-Hoops, electronic Pet Rocks, things of little more than passing fancy. But the minority that survive fickle consumer affection will go on to change our lives in ways that will make the social impact of PCs, VCRs, videocams and Walkmans pale by comparison.

Decades of electronic innovation have led us to use the term "revolution" lightly, but the revolution to come will not be forgotten anytime soon. A citizen was able to record the police beating of Rodney King in 1991 because by then the average videocam had more computing horsepower than an IBM 360 mainframe in its prime a decade earlier. Now we are packaging far greater power into utterly new kinds of information appliances, and the consequences are certain to transform our lives and society in utterly unexpected ways. It would be presumptuous to compare Newton to its 17th-century namesake, but the collective impact of this revolution in the making—and the machine that triggered it—might just be remembered for a century or two.

by FLYING

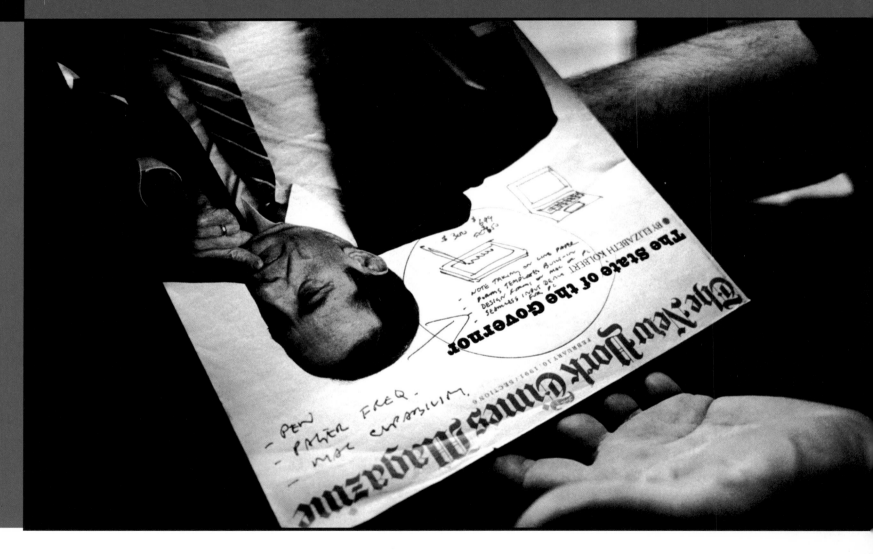

Crawling south from San Francisco on Highway 101 was the world's slowest taxi. At least that is what it seemed to the three fidgeting, airport-bound Appleniks inside. Michael Tchao, CJ Maupin and Michael Witlin had been invited to fly to Japan with their CEO, John Sculley, to work in-flight on his February 1991 Macworld Tokyo address. And they were running late.

Keeping the chairman of Apple Computer waiting for an overseas flight is nerve-wracking—and there was already enough tension to go around in the cab. Tchao, a twenty-seven-year-old Apple marketing specialist, was anxious about making a risky pitch to Sculley—a bold proposal he had been agonizing over for months. Now he found himself bothered by second thoughts.

"CJ, should I still do it?" Tchao asked Maupin, Sculley's principal speech writer.

"Yeah, do it. You should do it!" came her reply.

For weeks now, Maupin had been coaching and encouraging Tchao to lay out his idea for a new product that could radically affect Apple's future. She knew that Tchao was preparing to go over the head of his immediate superior at Apple—the sometimes mercurial Larry Tesler—and appeal directly to

ALTHOUGH Newton had been in development for several years, it was aboard Mike Markkula's private jet in February 1991 that Newton was "productized," Sculley's word for the moment when an R&D concept becomes real. During a flight to Tokyo, in a discussion with Michael Tchao, Sculley sketched out a downsized version of Newton, and listed a few key features on the cover of the *New York Times Magazine*. The Newton was reborn.

PRODUCT Marketing Manager Michael Tchao was the first marketing person to join the Newton project, in 1990 when he was twenty-six years old. He developed an immediate rapport with engineer Steve Capps, and they worked closely together to reconfigure the promising technologies being developed at the time into a compact, consumer-oriented product.

Sculley. But she believed in Tchao's ideas and knew her calming support would strengthen Tchao's resolve. He feared the move could cost him his job if the news got back to Tesler, head of a secretive group working on a new technology called "Newton."

Although job security was not a chief concern for someone as young, bright and talented as Tchao, he still wanted to keep his job. Apple had been his only employer since graduating from Stanford University six years earlier. The company snatched him up just a few hours after he set up camp in the corporate headquarters' lobby and staked out the personnel director, who was already familiar with his work from his days as a star summer intern. Tchao knew Apple well and had seen that it generally encouraged risk-taking and dissent and espoused a "buy-in" management style. But the product idea he wanted to propose to Sculley had already been rejected summarily by Tesler. Tchao knew that approaching Sculley would be a politically hazardous move, but he was at the end of his rope. He had been frustrated for months by a lack of company support for his idea. Now he was going to go for it. If only they could get to the airport.

They were late, but no matter. Sculley and his daughter, Laura, did not arrive until a few minutes later. Relief.

The flight crew at San Jose International Airport greeted the Apple party as they entered A.C. "Mike" Markkula, Jr.'s private plane, a three-jet Falcon 900 that was placed at Sculley's disposal. Markkula, an Apple board member and its former chief executive, had helped create the company back in 1977 by investing his own money and securing venture capital for co-founders Steven Jobs and Stephen Wozniak. Six years later, Markkula had been instrumental in persuading Sculley to quit his job as president of PepsiCo's soft-drink division to lead Apple.

Markkula's sleek jet was perfect for work or play. There were plush seats and a wood-paneled interior in the conversation area up front, a conference table in the middle and a bedroom in back with a VCR and tape library. An AppleTalk connection was built into every seat throughout the plane, allowing passengers to network their computers to each other or to connect to the LaserWriter printer on board.

Sculley had invited Tchao, Maupin and Witlin, an events coordinator, to join him on the private flight to help with his presentation to the Macworld

computer industry product convention. But he was also taking precautions. Under normal circumstances, the assembled team would have flown commercially. But the United States was at war in the Persian Gulf and Americans were anticipating attacks. The threat of terrorism was suddenly dictating the pulse and style of business throughout the world.

Shortly after take-off, Maupin broke out her new video recorder and, unaware that the microphone was catching her every utterance, started taking typical novice shots of feet and out-of-focus faces. She and Witlin mugged for the camera and headed to the cockpit to film a deadpanning pilot pretending to be lost. Nearby, a restless Tchao looked for his break to speak with Sculley. Normally animated, he was now hyperkinetic.

Maupin and Witlin started sorting slides and going over preparations for the Tokyo conference the following day; Laura Sculley was asleep in the bedroom. Tchao wanted uninterrupted time with the boss, for what people at Apple refer to as "mindshare." As Sculley looked through the Sunday *New York Times* at the conference table, Tchao saw his chance. He whispered to Maupin: "I'm going to go back and try and talk to John."

"Okay. We won't bother you."

Tchao ventured over to the table, greeted Sculley nervously and began his pitch. As he entered familiar territory, his anxiety dissipated. Sculley warmed quickly to the conversation and gave Tchao his full attention. After all, he carried with him a business card that read "John Sculley, Chief Listener," and he tried to live up to the role. Besides, Sculley was fond of Tchao and likely saw in him the driven, young marketing whiz he had been during his early years at PepsiCo. Sculley had recommended nine months earlier that Tchao join the research-oriented Newton group. Now he was eager for a progress report.

Tchao quickly reviewed the Newton group's work. The boss was already well-briefed on what was being done in the hypersecret research laboratory housed in a converted warehouse on Bubb Road in Cupertino, California. **An elite team of Apple engineers, many of whom had helped create the Apple II and Macintosh computers, had been working there since 1987 to come up with the next generation of breakthrough technology.** Tesler had been leading the engineers' group for nearly a year, and his product goal was to develop a laptop-sized, pen-based, multipurpose machine using a high-level coding language. The machine would do the standard work of a computer but also would boast extended communications abilities and, if not strictly artificial intelligence, a way to figure out users' needs. Tesler's idea was to make a new machine that would do everything a personal computer did and then some, with all its functions consolidated on a flat tablet that might resemble a gadget out of *Star Trek*.

Tchao described to Sculley some of the group's achievements that the engineers liked to call "cool"—for example, handwriting recognition that could turn written cursive into typeface and a wireless communication system using radio waves. The technologies were promising and the group was forging ahead slowly, but Tesler's envisioned product was not targeted to any specific market and would probably take a few more years to develop. Originally slated to retail at a prohibitive $8,000, its price was later revised to $4,000, and then to a high-end personal computer price point of around $2,000. It was a monster in a box.

It was a sore point for Tchao and his friend Steve Capps, a lead Newton engineer, that Tesler considered them subversive because they did not believe such an elaborate and expensive computing and communicating tool, despite its unparalleled capabilities, could immediately find a mass market—or, for that matter, any market at all. The two argued that the price and size of Tesler's currently planned product would categorize it strictly as a personal computer, making it part of a market that was already becoming saturated rapidly. They knew that Newton could be unique and that some of its advanced technologies, if combined within a product that was not specifically a computer, would be something altogether new.

Their idea—which Tesler rejected—was to market something small, something handheld. An inexpensive, quickly produced consumer product that would create a new market. **Newton would be revolutionary in its simplicity.** It would intelligently assist its users by learning their preferences and understanding their organization and communication needs, which would be conveyed in simple language with the nontechnical words used in daily life. The technology would be self-contained in a compact, unintimidating device that would emulate electronically the tools people already used on a daily basis: pen and paper.

Sitting at the conference table, Tchao talked and Sculley quickly sketched the young man's description of this new, intriguing, scaled-down

Newton product on the cover of that day's *New York Times Magazine*. As an upside-down New York Governor Mario Cuomo stared up at Sculley, Tchao gave a passionate pitch, spinning images of an intelligent mini-machine that would be unlike any other, in which pager and fax machine could all be integrated in a smart, accessible unit that could understand simple English—or French, German, Japanese—and could decipher handwriting. Size and price were to be kept to a minimum. Tchao was describing a stripped-down version of Tesler's Newton, an intelligent appliance that would "capture, organize and communicate" ideas and data. Something that would work the way people do. No keyboards or commands. No technical training required. It would be an electronic, digitized piece of note paper that could be scribbled on and that would be smart enough to interpret the meaning of the scribbles. The young man emphasized that he was not proposing to scrap Tesler's machine. All the same, he felt that opening the market to a family of future Newton devices would be possible only if the company developed the radically different mini-Newton—which Tesler opposed so strongly that he never considered selling the idea to the chairman.

Sculley's sketch was a perfect example of how Newton could prove useful. People routinely reach for a piece of paper or a bar napkin or a Post-it to jot down a phone number or draw an idea. But how was Sculley going to pass on or clean up his original drawing? Would he have to photocopy the magazine? Fold the periodical and put it in his jacket pocket until he had an opportunity to re-draw his concept? Run the ten-inch-by-twelve-inch magazine cover through a fax machine?

Along with his drawing of how this new, smaller Newton product might look, Sculley jotted down a number of points on technical, marketing and manufacturing goals: "Pen-based, pager frequency, Mac-capability." Sculley thought it would make sense to base this new machine on the same microprocessor chip used by the Macintosh.

Sculley was fascinated by Tchao's proposal. He recognized in it a consumer version of a portable product he had envisioned four years earlier—a notebook-sized machine he had dubbed the "Knowledge Navigator," which would offer users a form of artificial intelligence through an "agent." The agent would serve essentially as a screen-based secretary that would know its user's routine and information needs and that would allow them to communicate with one another. But Sculley told Tchao that he still needed evidence to back up what he himself suspected and Tchao believed: that the mini-Newton would be a commercial success and could be the first, industry standard-setting product of its kind.

The second idea Tchao presented to Sculley was to license Newton technologies broadly, in order to create a constant revenue stream for the company. He argued that Newton would be ideal for this type of licensing because it would be a brand-new consumer product that could be distributed through commercial channels, unlike most regular computers. This idea, while not new, appealed to Sculley.

Tchao left his meeting with the boss knowing they would talk again soon. His idea for an affordable Newton product, the size of a transistor radio with some of the futuristic Knowledge Navigator's functionality, seemed to click for Sculley. **As those close to him well knew, there are different stages of product development in Sculley's mind, and one of the hardest for new, untested technologies to achieve is to become what he calls "productized"—an inelegant word he coined to describe the leap from the possible to the producible.** Productizing the Newton was a process in full-swing on the flight to Tokyo.

Barely able to contain his excitement, a grinning Tchao rushed back to Witlin and Maupin. Only once had Maupin gotten up to see how the meeting was progressing, just long enough to point the camera and shoot Tchao and Sculley together and add gravely to the videotape voice track: "A very important high-level strategy session here." Barely into the trip, Tchao had captured Sculley's imagination and made the chairman's long-term vision momentarily manifest. All before the in-flight fettucini was served.

The excitement level was up as the jet approached the appropriately named Cold Bay, Alaska, a refueling stop in the Aleutian Islands. A solitary Quonset hut that served as the airport terminal was the only sign of humanity at the edge of a tarmac overshadowed by an adjacent snow-capped mountain. Maupin started filming and then took still photos of Sculley smiling in front of the hut's Coke machine as he held up a copy of a science magazine called *Odyssey*, the only periodical in the hut's sparsely filled book rack. Ironically, it was also the title of Sculley's autobiography. Everyone laughed at the set-up. After all, Pepsi—not Coke—was not only the choice of a new generation, but also was Sculley's previous employer. Whether out of

SPEECH writer for John Sculley and other Apple execs, CJ Maupin joined Michael Tchao and Michael Witlin, along with Sculley and his daughter, Laura, aboard a flight to Macworld Tokyo. She has helped develop and script many key Apple product introductions.

6 7

deference to the boss or the result of an informal taste test, the unwritten cola-drinking rule at Apple is "No Coke . . . Pepsi, Pepsi, Pepsi." The mood was light despite the oppressively cold Alaskan winter.

Taxi and take-off were smooth, and the jet climbed to cruising speed and altitude and began a path following the circumference of the Pacific Rim. Aviation maps on which the United States is not centered show clearly how far California and the West Coast are from the Old World and how close they are to Pacific trade routes. Business links between Asia and California are long-standing and Sculley's vision of Apple's business construction for the next millennium included building many more bridges to Japan and its rapidly developing region. **The flight to Japan was every bit as much a trip to Apple's future.**

Worlds away, the United States was leading an international effort to destroy the leadership structure and service infrastructure of a country once known as the cradle of civilization. Iraq and its primary military technology sponsor, the Soviet Union, were being shown the inferiority of their strategies and systems in graphic detail. Twenty-four-hour war coverage on CNN made the world familiar with the language of "smart" technology and showed that a programmed missile could be precise enough to guide itself down the ventilation system of a building before detonating a bomb. Suddenly, everyone got a crash-course in microprocessing at work and the superiority of American technology. It was a brutal and expensive lesson, in human and environmental terms, and one that could not be misunderstood: Whoever controls technology controls the future.

Business parallels the work of nations, following paths of both diplomacy and warfare. Sculley was heading to Japan not only to present a keynote address at Macworld, but also to make progress in his search for alliances with Japanese consumer electronics industry superpowers. He believed that the convergence of computer, consumer electronic, entertainment and information-based industries was inevitable and that it would create a new, as yet undefined market too large for any single company to handle. Three and one-half trillion dollars was how he figured it—and a big chunk of that would be up for grabs when the market was ripe.

Sculley wanted to position Apple at the head of the pack once it came time to grab. His strategy was to lay the groundwork in Japan by forming early alliances with Japanese companies. Going to war head-on with these powerhouses would be as foolhardy as it would be expensive. He wanted to enlist them instead in a symbiotic business relationship and form a new, international *keiretsu* (a Japanese word used to describe joint-venture bonded corporations—bonded with superglue) that still would allow for competition and lateral movement.

Sculley's plans for the *keiretsu* were part of his vision for Apple, but he was aware of broader implications and had his Tokyo-bound passengers hard at work refining his message. Tchao and Maupin busied themselves pulling together the presentation on a Macintosh Classic with Tchao seated at the terminal and clicking the mouse to glide from slide to slide.

Tchao read aloud:

"John Sculley, Chairman and CEO presenting . . . Architecture for a new age vision."

Tchao's voice took on a slow, momentous tone as Maupin watched over his shoulder and listened to her carefully crafted words.

"We are entering a whole new era, a decade of positive change. **Around the world, organizations have realized that you cannot intimidate people into productivity.** The key is to let people do what they do best in whatever way works best for them. At the same time, the past principles of mass production will give ordinary people access to powerful technology. What was affordable to the few, becomes available to the many. Mass production becomes mass productivity. The industrial revolution meets the age of technology. The walls have come down . . . ."

Maupin joined Tchao and they spoke in unison:

"The only limits will be the size of your ideas and the degree of your dedication."

A dramatic pause.

"People: This is an exciting time to be alive."

Unlike most travelers or products coming to Japan from the United States, the Apple entourage, landing at Tokyo's Narita Airport, did not have to go through customs, but instead was ushered immediately into a couple of limousines and taken straight to the luxury Hotel Ikura, where a deep-bowing, eight-man receiving line welcomed Sculley.

The Apple chairman's comportment seems less alien to Japanese executives than the behavior of some of his American business colleagues. An innately shy person who offers few overt emotional signals, Sculley requires time to trust and relax with strangers. Patience and planning are the keys to doing business in an environment that many consider hostile to foreigners; some are lucky enough to have those characteristics without having to affect them.

Tchao, trying hard to concentrate on his Macworld duties, knew his Newton work had just begun. When he got a moment alone, he picked up the phone and reported back to his buddy Capps: "I finally broke down and told John—and he really likes the idea. We gotta start doing this." The thrill of receiving Sculley's positive feedback was hard to maintain because Tchao knew that from now on, his obligations would be—as he would repeatedly say in dry tones—"all-consuming and very challenging." Sculley's Macworld address was warmly received and, as with each of his regular trips to Japan, his links to companies there strengthened, and now they would be heading home with a victory he could ponder.

As Tchao took his return-flight seat behind the pilot in the private jet, he noted the other planes around him. An aviation buff since childhood, Tchao was awed by the grandeur of the Boeing 747. Now, a couple of days after he had presented his idea to Sculley, he sat again on the Narita Airport runway in Markkula's Falcon 900, dwarfed by the nearly one hundred surrounding jumbo jets, a minnow amidst the whales.

The Apple plane's "auto-pilot" device indicated a malfunction and caused a long departure delay. When the plane carrying both Apple personnel and hopes for the freshly productized Newton finally left Japan and swooshed back home, its course in the dark night sky would have to be manually adjusted.

Now, if the Newton concept Tchao and Capps proposed was to become manifest—with Apple entering a new consumer electronics market, broadly licensing its technologies and actively seeking new international business partners—the company, too, would be moving quickly forward without its auto-pilot, charting an unfamiliar course to a distant future.

Landing in Anchorage at 3:00 a.m., passengers and possessions were pulled off the plane for a U.S. Customs inspection. Home, sweet home. An immigration official turned to Tchao and, pointing to Sculley, asked, "Are you two related?" Tchao found the question amusing, wondering how anyone could possibly mistake a Chinese-American like himself as Sculley's kin.

"Yeah, he's my father."

Sculley smiled at Tchao: "Son."

RE-- EVOLUTION

1 9 8 5 - 1 9 8 9

LARRY Kenyon, at right, joined the Newton team as a networking specialist and is working on a problem with Michael Culbert, who developed sound software for Newton.

0 1

Jobs, the revolutionary, wanted to change the world by putting a personal computer in every home. He wanted Sculley, the marketing master who had created the Pepsi Generation, to whip up demand for Apple computers, and, in the process, take the company to new heights. He lured Sculley away from PepsiCo in 1983, and together they made a formidable team for two years. Their eventual falling-out was as wrenching for the company as it was for the men themselves. Apple would suffer the repercussions of the rift for years to come.

Although the circumstances surrounding Jobs' resignation may still be fuel for debate, his role in developing the personal computer is indisputable. The technology he introduced to mass markets has truly changed the way people work and play. **Personal computers became tools that spurred revolutionary change in society, bringing data and information technology to both homes and workplaces.** Renting videos, checking out books from the library or purchasing groceries became governed by automated scanning devices that allowed for inventory control, accurate price changes and, in the worst case, unauthorized glimpses of private individual behavior and proclivities.

But the technology, with the exception of VCR programming, became facile and as much a part of the unobtrusive modern background as the radio. Americans coming of age now are scarcely able to remember a time before Ronald Reagan's presidency and the existence of the personal computer. Garages and attics now contain old monitors, keyboards and disk-drive units that already look as quaint as the hand tools or wood-frame tennis rackets sharing the same storage space.

Jobs' revolution introduced two tools for the mind. The Apple II was the first such tool. The Macintosh was the second. Jobs provided the zeal, spirit and vision to create both desktop personal computers. If anyone doubted that he had revolutionary goals no less modest than Lenin's, then all one had to do was watch Superbowl XVIII, between the Los Angeles Raiders and the Washington Redskins, when a million-dollar commercial came on with a good-versus-evil attack on bureaucratic Big Brother: "On January 24, Apple Computer will announce Macintosh . . . 1984 won't be like *1984*." Subtle? No. Effective? Yes.

Jobs' vision of future digital technologies, industry insiders argued, occluded his perspective of the fiduciary realities of a growing company. He saw clearly the potential social payoffs of personal computing, but after Apple went public, Jobs seemed unwilling to accommodate Wall Street's addictive need for a company that sustained quarterly and long-term financial growth. After a series of bad inventory, manufacturing, advertising and product-cannibalizing decisions in 1985, Apple—until then the fastest-growing company in U.S. business history and an established Fortune 500 member—showed its first quarterly loss ever. Sculley, who had been steadily consolidating his own power, had to make tough decisions.

In the reorganization that ensued, Jobs departed and jobs evaporated. On June 14, 1985, one-fifth of Apple's workforce was sacked. **To the 4,600 employees who remained, it was a slap in the face to find out that Apple was as much a business as it was a cult.** Morale dropped lower than the California water tables.

During those difficult days, engineer Steve Sakoman, watching from the sidelines, felt it was "an insane time at Apple, a somewhat psychotic place." A hardware specialist from Hewlett-Packard, Sakoman had come to Cupertino in 1984 to work on MacPhone, an early Macintosh-telephone interface that AT&T and Apple were interested in developing jointly. Sakoman had arrived at Apple

PROGRAMMER Bob Welland signed on to the Newton team to help design and develop the operating system. He is taking five with fellow programmers Phil Beisel, left, and Scott Douglass, at right.

with high hopes. Bored and restless after completing work on Hewlett-Packard's first portable computer, Sakoman craved greater creativity: "I saw myself building DOS clones for the rest of my life. I thought Apple might be more fun."

While there was seldom a dull moment with Jobs around, Apple's entertainment quotient dipped after his displacement. Motivating the stunned remaining staff was a tough task for Sakoman, who was put in charge of the Apple II and Macintosh hardware groups. He shared the task with his boss, Macintosh's new general manager, Jean-Louis Gassée, a flamboyant, diamond-stud-sporting mathematician who had been brought to California after running Apple's French division.

There was little time for reflection during the post-Jobs fight for survival, as the Apple engineers were thrust into one immediate challenge after another. But after the successful February 1987 introduction of the powerful Macintosh II, a computer that dramatically increased Apple's market share, the engineering teams found a moment to pause and reflect on their work. Sakoman, feeling a sense of *déjà vu*, was once again in a creative dilemma: "I saw myself in the position of doing Mac clones for the rest of my life and that didn't sound like very much fun."

Like others in Silicon Valley that year, Sakoman decided it might be time to strike out on his own, grab some readily available venture capital and pursue his own vision: to research and develop a computer that was completely different from anything on the market at the time. Years earlier, while at Hewlett-Packard, Sakoman had enjoyed spending his spare time toying with "hand-entry" devices, machines without keyboards. He found data-entry machines awkward and believed that "It's an accident of history that computers are the way they are—that we bang on them." He knew that pen and paper were the simplest and most natural tools people used to capture thoughts, and he had always wanted to experiment further with what he called his "bootleg project."

He confided in Gassée that he was looking to get out of Apple. Tired of the trade-offs and politics involved in corporate projects, he was going to start his own company where he would be free to research his own ideas about what a computer should be. But Gassée's influence had grown at Apple in the past couple of years, and now, as head of new-product development, he was able to make Sakoman a tempting offer: Would he stay if Gassée could create an independent unit within Apple?

Sakoman considered the difficulties involved with research and development—the "corporate immune system," he called it—and came back to Gassée, saying he might be interested, but only if Gassée met his conditions that the new product group had "to be outside the normal channels, to be as independent as possible, to feel as much like a start-up as possible." Sakoman was also adamant that his group be kept away from the sullying influence of marketers, because "marketing people in general have a lot nearer-term focus. Their wheels are spinning on how am I going to sell this today, how am I going to fit it into the current product line, price points, distribution. In my mind at that time, this was not compatible with what the job at hand was, which was to rethink what a personal computer would be. I didn't want that type of marketing thinking." If Gassée could keep the rest of the company entirely away from Sakoman's group, or at least hold it greatly at bay, then it was a deal. Gassée agreed to provide an environment that allowed for pure, unrestricted research where engineers were to feel uninhibited and unconstrained by market pressures. By no means, he assured Sakoman, would marketing people be allowed to enter and defile the holy temple of the scientific priesthood. Sakoman, aware that the option of leaving his job and developing a start-up company was fraught with its own perils and compromises, shook Gassée's hand and closed the deal. He dusted off a code-name he had been saving for just the right project: Newton.

Sakoman chose Newton not only because the original Apple Computer logo depicted the 17th-century English scientist sitting beneath an apple tree, but mainly because he believed that "Newton shook up people's ideas about the way things are."

Holed up in a spare corner on the top floor of the corporate headquar-

"Visiting the Newton building was kind of like visiting the Media Lab [at MIT]. The building on Bubb Road was away from the rest of the company, very high security, and inside were some of the best and brightest engineers in the company—all working on this team on different research projects. And it was kind of, the sky's the limit. There weren't a lot of money constraints on what kind of hardware the software could run on, and there was some really neat stuff happening." — JAMES JOAQUIN

ters' executive Mahogany Row, Sakoman concocted his plans. He wanted "to start extremely small, stay small and grow in a very controlled way" because he believed products reflect the values of their creators, and he wanted those values to be readily apparent to users. He found an empty warehouse on Bubb Road, a couple of miles away from Apple's main campus, and planned to move his group there by the end of 1987.

Inside the suspended-ceilinged offices of the Bubb Road warehouse were chin-high cubicles that broke up the floor space to make it look like a rat's maze. Within a few months, these cubicles would contain the big cheeses of Newton software and hardware development—engineers who had earned the respect of their peers and gained the distinction of having shipped products "out the door."

Hiring staff was a breeze for Sakoman because "when there's something new, it's always easy to recruit." He approached talented, experienced engineers one by one and gave his sales pitch: "We have to wipe the slate clean. Typing on a keyboard isn't a natural thing. Most people never learn it and the people who do learn it don't learn it until quite a few years into their existence. But grabbing a pencil and pointing with it and scribbling and making marks is a skill that you learn really early, and therefore it feels a lot more natural.

"Why can't we write things the way we were taught to in school? Why can't the computer deal with things that we're not good at? When we draw a square, we ought to be able to look at it and say, 'That's a square.' A computer ought to be more natural, it ought to be more directly manipulated, it ought to make much more of an effort to do what you meant instead of what you did. All those are very hard things."

His first recruits signed up quickly. Finding solutions for "very hard things" is exactly what excites engineers; a challenge gets the juices flowing. Problem-solving defines their existence. Pete Foley took the lead in designing hardware, and Glen Adler was responsible for helping to find a graphics tablet, the electronic slate that could be written on directly with a pen-like device. The team then looked for someone in software. Steve Capps, who had been a member of Jobs' original Macintosh group, was the man they wanted.

LEAD Software Engineer Steve Capps takes a break from programming and plays a Jaminator, the toy he invented that enables its user to play perfect solos along with rock-and-roll hits such as The Rolling Stones' "Start Me Up." May 1993.

5   8

A software engineer with a near-rock-star legendary status in the software development community, Capps looks unassuming and unaffected. A self-proclaimed "software nerd," he is distinguished not by the shorts that nearly all true software engineers consider standard issue, but by his footwear. In a gathering of junk-food-eating, compile-conversing, nocturnal programmers, he looks more like a big, long-haired skateboarder, wearing laceless, sleek, checkerboard-patterned Vans tennis shoes. Nothing comes between him and his Vans, not even meetings with suit-and-tie-clad executives from other corporations.

When the core Newton team approached Capps, he was busy building his own music software company and inventing a new guitar-synthesizer instrument. They told him about the new, great machine they wanted to develop, one with not only a pen interface but advanced communications abilities too, all in a lightweight package. Sakoman emphasized that Newton would be the next new productivity tool and that portability would be important because "tools, to be useful, have to be with you. Unless a tool's accessible, it's worthless."

Capps listened to the pitch and expressed his major concern: "I don't

"In our group, one thing I set out to do was to make sure nobody experienced the kind of interview process I went through, and another was to make sure that the group started to take a more open-minded view of bringing people in who would have different points of view—because we're creating consumer products here—not Macs that are going to go on desktops in the hands of people who are very technical, or people who are business oriented." — DONNA AUGUSTE

want to make a yuppie toy." Creating a Newton with everything on it, he argued, meant that they could not hold the price. A dash of communications, a pinch of longhand-written mathematical formula recognition and solution capabilities plus a dollop of network connecting power would all certainly add up to a beefy cost. This new gadget, he feared, was doomed to be a product that would be available only to those who could afford expensive consumer toys.

Sakoman convinced Capps that his goal was to promote pure research—"wipe the slate clean" became his mantra—not yuppie-toy production, and that the results of this research would be a product riding the leading edge of technology, something useful in both education and business. The work of the Newton group would remain top secret. The team would be physically separated from the rest of the company, and pure in spirit through its isolation from marketing specialists. Sakoman and Gassée guaranteed it. Capps was hooked.

Mike Culbert, the fifth person to join the engineers-without-portfolio team, arrived in March 1988, four months after its formation. He had fled what he considered the "rigid environment" of AT&T, where he worked on network interfaces and digital switches while finishing his graduate degree at Cornell University.

Culbert is one of those rare single-career people. "Ever since I was a new-born kid I've been an electrical engineer." As a child, Culbert used to play with extension cords and gleefully take apart his parents' electric coffee makers. "One day, I decided that I wanted to learn how the dishwasher worked, so I disassembled the entire dishwasher. At age nine, I was very good at disassembling things but not so good at putting them back together again." Fortunately for both his parents and his future employers, Culbert's skills improved.

Although the AT&T defector joined Newton four months after the others, he was able to contribute to early discussions of the group's goals. The team brainstormed as Culbert asked defining questions: "Okay, we've got this fun computer called Macintosh. What do we do next? What is the next computing device that is going to be interesting in the industry?" In their rarefied research environment, they were asking engineering questions rather than trying to respond to consumer needs. So perhaps it was little surprise when their initial goal turned out to be an engineer's dream and a consumer's nightmare. In 1988, the Newton group was researching the ultimate $8,000 machine. Meanwhile, although the price of the Macintosh remained relatively high, the price of competing multi-megabyte, Intel-based DOS machines like the powerful, ubiquitous IBM-clones used in many offices was dipping below $1,000. In a cloistered state, the Newton group was busy putting together an engineer's fantasy without any idea of where the market was going.

Culbert used a lover's terms of endearment to describe the Newton's technical appeal: "Tall, dark, sensuous, a two-processor machine based around Hobbit that had a 720 X 560, active matrix, gray-scale screen, a huge number of pixels, very fine pixel pitch. It had a magnetic tablet behind the screen, and it had a wireless local area network, using spread spectrum infrared, radio frequency technology. Very expensive, high-end."

It was a processing Porsche, a "no-compromise" machine about which Culbert could coo endlessly. "It was quite impressive; the product ran for approximately ten hours on a single battery charge, and had the speed of about two-and-a-half Macintosh II FXs. The final product was about the size of an eight-and-a-half-by-eleven sheet of paper, and very thin. We were looking at about three-quarters of an inch."

Gassée the aesthete strove to inspire innovation and technological progress by creating and protecting this research haven for his small group of highly talented engineers. More team members came aboard as the Newton machine gained greater functionality and added hardware. The Gallic godfather's indulgence and patronage gave the Newton engineers the impression that they were his "golden boys." But Newton was as undirected as it was protected. Capps thought of it as the graduate school he never attended, but "without any actual tests, no requirements or anything." He found the environment downright leisurely. "We were all coasting, there's no doubt about it, but that's what you're meant to do in research. You're meant to sit around and think, and you go, 'Hey, that's a neat, shiny problem.'"

Based on his previous experience in developing the Macintosh, Capps voiced a desire "to see if we could do a project without killing ourselves." He also felt strongly that "I didn't want everybody to turn into assholes, and it was just an important thing not to forget you had a life. When I first started, I refused to work after 10:00 p.m. So you'd work 10:00 a.m. to 10:00 p.m. They were normal hours for us."

With all that spare time on his hands, Capps turned some of his attention

to the decor of the team's work space, outlining a newt in freshly poured concrete and spray-painting the Bubb warehouse's outside walls with foot-high, black-and-orange newts. Sakoman could only understand the added decoration as an improvement, since he felt the architect had designed the warehouse renovations "to punish me, by making everything purple—my least favorite color—down to the flowers outside."

Creating the Newton team and moving it to the building on Bubb Road were rebellious acts marking the first step in a pattern that those who had been at Apple long enough could identify all too easily. A small, internal start-up project begins, then raises the pirate flag against Apple as a company and, finally, emerges dominant. It had happened with the Macintosh, to the detriment of the Apple II.

Partly because Apple had achieved success through risk-taking, it had a reputation as an enormously innovative company. Less apparent to those outside was that with its success, Apple had also become a big corporation with a large, entrenched bureaucracy that was overwhelmingly dependent on the Macintosh. Now a corporate megalith, Apple had succumbed to the same inertia it once ridiculed in other bigger, bluer-chip companies.

Physically distant but enveloped by Apple's corporate aura, the Newton crew set about trying to make the Bubb building their home. They had some ideas about how to make their space more comfortable and conducive to creativity. However, there were set ways of requisitioning that were alien to a small start-up. When Sakoman wanted to add a basketball rim to the side of the building, the company made him jump through legal hoops before approving the request. Then, when he wanted to take away cubicles and give engineers small, private offices surrounding a common area with couches for lounging and informal brainstorming, he was told that Apple did not "do offices." His idea to design a different, perhaps more efficient, workspace had to be kicked up directly to Sculley for approval. If Sakoman wanted to buy hardware from a company other than Apple, he first needed to check with his own company's hardware groups for supplies and then had to fight for them to prioritize his request. Often this task seemed impossible as he competed for attention with the Apple product groups that were actually bringing in revenue.

In 1989, the second year of the project, Sakoman spent much of his time "selling our continued existence" to the company. Gassée dictated most of Newton's existence, but bureaucratic machinations at Apple could grind down executive decisions made by fiat. Gassée told the rest of the company simply to give Newton resources and then leave it alone. But Sakoman had to take care of the details involved in actually procuring those resources and justifying Newton's isolation. His work became increasingly thankless as the rest of the company's prejudice against Newton grew obvious. Employees outside Newton had become suspicious of the unknown. A scorched-earth policy of product development was the company tradition, a Jobs legacy. It was even a stated Sculley goal that a modern company should make its own products obsolete. As a result, there was an unspoken fear throughout Apple that Newton would devour the Macintosh, just as the Mac had gobbled up the groundbreaking Apple II.

Sakoman tried bravely to maintain the Gassée-promised separation of Newton's church from the Apple state. As time passed, though, he got tired of the balancing act and the struggle to protect Newton. Gassée was a loyal patron, but Sakoman wearied of trying to satisfy other reluctant benefactors at the management level while keeping his own little team unaware of conflict. As the liaison responsible for representing Newton to the rest of Apple, he had to allay the company's fears that Newton, like the Macintosh group before, might "raise the pirate flag. But there's a fine line between being open and spending your whole life doing demos." He resented "the religion" at Apple, and "the religion," as Sakoman likes to say irreverently, "is Macintosh." To any in-house paranoid or fanatic (and there were plenty of both in those days), Sakoman's Newton team could be seen as a cult of blasphemers aiming not merely to reform, but to revolt.

Sakoman finally revolted against the bureaucracy that had thwarted his original goal to run a genuinely independent start-up. He quit. Gassée, for other reasons, had also had enough—and the feeling was mutual; Apple had had more than enough of him. **By spring 1990, both the Newton group's leader and its patron were gone. Uncertainty reigned. It was now open season on the freshly orphaned group.**

AMONG the mementos found in John Sculley's office are pink sneakers from the PINK software development project, along with family pictures and other prized possessions.

5 1

At about the same time the Newton group was wondering if it had a future, Sculley was hatching plans to reinvent his personal computer company—and the entire marketplace.

During the late 1980s, Sculley had been at Apple's helm through a period of constant readjustment. Company-wide reorganizations seemed to come more frequently than the seasons. Readjustments continued into the early months of 1990, with executives changing job titles as regularly as the original Macintosh 128K changed disks. When Apple was not foundering, it simply was coasting. It was not directionless, just lethargic. The summer of 1990 was a time to face the dissonant music from a band of one-note Wall Street analysts and investment advisors, whose rap included a refrain that Apple had to work on increasing its market share.

Sculley and company heard the market's call and reacted by producing a slew of low-cost Macintoshes in the fall, including both the Classic and the LC. Sculley's profile rose with the profits. Now a multibillion-dollar Fortune 500 company, Apple bought itself time with money earned from sales of its new, affordable machines. Cyclical gains certainly would allow Apple to survive— but in order to thrive, Sculley recognized that it needed a big win and a long-

IN October of 1990, John Sculley, CEO, led the press on a tour of the Macintosh factory in Fremont, California while introducing the first low-cost Macs, including the Macintosh Classic and LC. Consumers and Wall Street analysts were pleased that Apple finally answered their call for it to increase its market share by slashing prices.

"IN my years working with John, in all kinds of extremely stressful situations I have never seen him blow up or lose his focus on the task at hand," reflects Regis McKenna public relations executive Gabi Schindler. When a colleague mentioned Sculley's bow tie, he told him, "I wear them because I am one of the few people I know who can actually tie one," a skill he learned in prep school.

term strategy that would allow it to earn revenues from more than just the Mac.

Sculley knew that the only way technology companies—particularly Apple and other hardware manufacturers—would survive the 1990s would be to innovate both in technology and business strategies. **He realized that he had to train his company to win the technology sprint yet still survive the marathon.** But he also sensed that industry managers both inside and outside Apple were resisting more fundamental change. They were still getting "hung up on saying that future products and devices are just a logical extension of what computers are today. But they really are quite different."

Newton under Sakoman had the potential to be the ultimate personal computer when it was finally developed, but Sculley had become acutely aware that the market for personal computers was changing rapidly and that if all Apple did "was design hardware and become an assembler of that, there would not be enough profit margin." He foresaw that failed hardware companies would litter the roadside of future data highways like the wreckage of so many abandoned cars.

In order to spread the risks and share the costs of future hardware

JOHN Sculley departs a meeting with the Newton product marketing group, led by Manager Michael Tchao, center, and Product Line Manager for Software and Tools James Joaquin, left.

"I think there is impermanence in the new economic model—nothing is guaranteed longevity, whether it's a corporate structure or products in a company or people in a company. There's nothing negative about that. It just means people will come and grow and eventually move on to other things and then other people will come and grow and move on and the company will take one shape and then other shapes. ... Apple is right on the edge of that because so much of our company is about relationships with other companies."

— JOHN SCULLEY

development, Sculley's new strategy included entering into diverse partnerships, sometimes with perceived competitors. The ensuing "coopetition," both cooperating and competing with partner companies, he thought, could force Apple into greater efficiency and a shot at the big money—the massive brand-new market he estimated for inevitably convergent communications, consumer electronics and computer companies. Sculley saw that, as with companies like Microsoft or Intel, **"The real market value for the industry shifted from people who built computers to people who built the technology."**

Sculley wanted to move away from the business model of Apple's past—one based primarily on the development and marketing of Macintosh. For too many years, Apple had been milking this cash cow, and now it needed to come up with new sources of revenue from emerging but still-distant technologies that would propel the company into the 21st century. Competitive computer-market pressures were forcing profit margins in one steady direction: down. The recession-plagued U.S. economy was not helping matters.

Sculley thought that licensing should play a central role in his broad new business model. This, he believed, would make the most financial and

JOHN Sculley has been up and working for four hours when he arrives at his office at 7:00 a.m., where he pauses to read the morning paper.

JOHN Sculley checks into a Los Angeles hotel suite with his aides where he will meet to discuss alliances with IBM executives.

marketing sense. Although Sculley's proposed licensing strategy initially met with some resistance from management, he convinced skeptics that "by getting a broad number of licensees for the hardware, we'd have the chance to amortize our R&D investments across not only our unit growth, but also our partners' unit growth. Plus we'd get a chance to get some critical mass out there." In short, by licensing its software and hardware, Apple could set a standard for technology and reap the benefits.

Licensing was not a new issue at Apple. It just never had been a focal point of its business strategy. Sculley saw that Apple had the opportunity to wean itself from the stiffening competition of the hardware world by licensing its solely-owned, user-friendly Macintosh operating systems, an opportunity lost because of corporate indecision. Licensing the Mac systems could have fortified the computer maker with revenues from software—the closest thing there was to a renewable resource in the digital world. It also could have created a preferred standard operating system for most desktop machines if it had been properly marketed. Everyone in the industry had observed with envy how William Gates' Microsoft Corporation had built an empire through publishing and licensing operating systems—and that it had done so without

investing in developing expensive hardware systems. It was obvious that Microsoft did not make computers. It just made money.

The often-debated, low-risk decision to keep the Macintosh system exclusive to Apple would confine its market share. Apple watched as Microsoft produced and profited from a replicant Windows program for the more prevalent IBM and IBM-clone DOS-based machines. Microsoft had produced interface software that would go on to outsell its Macintosh fraternal twin by four and one half-to-one in 1992 unit sales.

Not wanting Apple to remain a closed-system company where Macintosh decisions directed and limited corporate decisions, Sculley set to work on changing the business. He told his company: "Let's build a completely different financial model . . . a value-chain model, which says that you've got to look at the entire value chain, in terms of where you can make your profits along the way."

The value chain's links looked strongest in the field of communications, an area that was growing ever more difficult to distinguish from the computer market. Sculley sought "to strengthen our relationships with telecommunications companies, to move more into services, and in fact, to expand the whole value chain, eventually bringing in hundreds of companies, each participating in some different way. If Apple can be at the core of all this, getting a little bit from each part of the value chain, that can be a tremendously valuable business to Apple shareholders."

Exploiting the value chain would be a way to take advantage of the impending integration of computers and communications that Sculley foresaw. It would move Apple away from what Sculley termed the "desktop" metaphor, in which computers are used primarily for spreadsheets and word processing, and toward a "conversation" metaphor, in which there would be greater interaction among users.

Communications were key to Sculley's vision of the future—a vision he first articulated in 1987 with a new technology he called the Knowledge Navigator: "The major catalysts in a Knowledge Navigator are communications and conversation, not computing and simulation, which is what computers were designed for." The Navigator was never a product, only a product goal, and for years, Sculley remained excited by the idea's potential. The Navigator would be capable of recognizing human speech and could be instructed by the user's voice and would respond in articulate, human speech.

To illustrate his idea, Sculley produced a slick, five-minute video showing a University of California at Berkeley professor talking to a simple screen that had no keyboard, no on/off switches, no disk drives. When spoken to, the screen popped up an "agent" of pleasant disposition and perfect comportment, a fresh-faced, thirtysomething, digital urban male professional, a DUMPY, who appeared in a postage-stamp position on the screen and guided his user through phone messages and information and data retrieval. In the video, the professor instructed the Knowledge Navigator to combine information on desert growth in Africa with facts about rainforest destruction in Latin America. The agent responded by comparing the data pictorially. The Knowledge Navigator had more important functions, too. It was also able to remind its user to call his mother.

The notion of a Knowledge Navigator was regarded as a fantastic piece of science fiction by many in the industry, but Sculley was convinced that future technological breakthroughs could create such a device. It was his vision that computers would develop into more than just an interface for people. He felt that users would want to use post-computer machines "as a window to pass through, which would allow them to communicate with other people—to communicate ideas and simulations, and to access information."

Like the Knowledge Navigator, Newton in 1990 was nothing more than a set of initially researched and slowly developing technologies. It was a drain on Apple's resources with no immediate promise of developing a marketable or profitable product. Newton team morale continued to sink steadily as the engineers realized that the secrecy that once protected their project had also kept others from knowing of its successes. Sculley was not ready to kill Newton, since he saw some of its technology as having descended from the Knowledge Navigator, but he had yet to be convinced of its viability. To his way of thinking, Newton's folio size, high price and double-processor-run functionality still defined it as little more than a personal computer. A new personal computer on steroids, perhaps, that differentiated itself only in that it featured a pen as an input device.

Aside from the general allure of Newton technology's licensing potential, Sculley was reluctant to pull the plug on the project because he was concerned that the Newton team talent might leave Apple. So he decided to dispatch his trusted technical lieutenant to conduct a review of Newton, to see what—if any—technologies were salvageable. In March of 1990 he sent over Larry Tesler.

"In some respects, the Newton team is really as close to the cultural model of the original Macintosh team as we have. On the other hand, I think it's wiser because it's a more experienced group of people. Most of the members of the original Macintosh team were in their early twenties and they'd never been in another company before. This time, we have people coming from the original Macintosh team—so they're ten years older—and we have people coming from other industries, who are bringing a more open perspective. The business model of the Macintosh was an outgrowth of the experience of the people who built the machine. They were just as talented a group, but because they were less experienced in worldly business their criteria was, 'Let's make it incredibly great.' They had to have a belief inside of themselves that they could do it better than anybody else in the world—and they probably did—but the consequence of that was that they chose not to rely on anyone else to do anything. They relied on themselves to do everything. That's a completely impractical approach in this age in which products have to be brought to market much faster, where you've got to be able to leverage across telecommunications and content development as well as device development.... The Macintosh model was a closed-loop system. This is an open system that is almost like a great, swirling cyclone that keeps pulling more stuff into it and gets bigger and bigger." — JOHN SCULLEY

JOHN Sculley gets made up for a live 3:00 a.m. interview on *CBS This Morning* at the CBS studios in Hollywood.

OF TRUTH

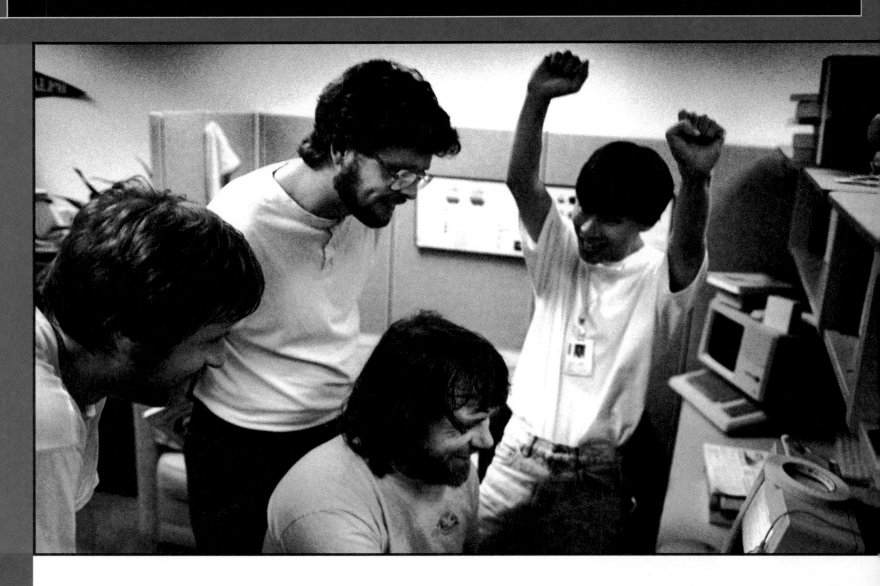

1990

ALEX Knight bangs his head on the table in not-so-mock frustration during a product marketing meeting. Alex, 27, was an early member of the Newton marketing team, hired by Michael Tchao, but left the project for Continuum, a company owned by Bill Gates in February 1993.

01 :

Tesler entered the hermetically sealed engineering environment thinking that he would probably extract the most promising Newton discoveries and developments and redistribute the inventive spoils around the company. Instead, what he found was so encouraging that in the end, he recommended the team and the technologies be kept intact. He saw the beginnings of a viable product that excited him so much, in fact, that he wanted to lead the group. Tesler reported directly to Sculley and his high-level access ultimately assured Newton's survival. He became Newton's savior.

Tesler was a brilliant engineer with twenty-nine years of experience in the computer business. He started out programming when he was in high school, worked as a software consultant in college, then moved to Stanford University's artificial intelligence laboratory in the mid-1960s. Pursuing his passion for research, he joined Xerox's legendary Palo Alto Research Center (PARC) in the 1970s. While at PARC, Tesler also worked on one of the first portable computers, but was disappointed with its sluggish pace of develop-

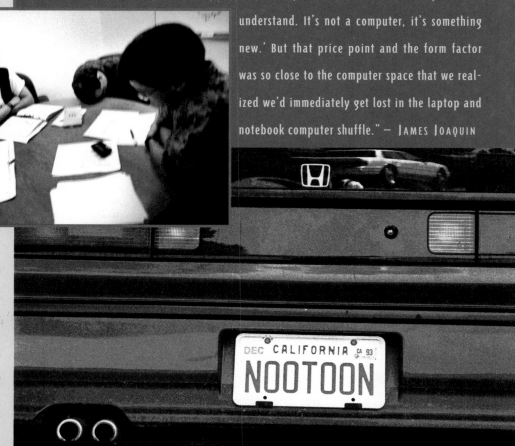

"We did a lot of focus groups with customers to find out what they really liked. Because we actually started with a larger form factor for Newton that had a lot of software features, but was very expensive, it put it into the price range of a computer. And when we described it to customers, when they heard the functionality and they heard the price, they said, 'Well, that costs about what my notebook computer costs, so then it should run Lotus 1-2-3 and WordPerfect, just like my notebook computer.' And we said, 'No, you don't understand. It's not a computer, it's something new.' But that price point and the form factor was so close to the computer space that we realized we'd immediately get lost in the laptop and notebook computer shuffle." — JAMES JOAQUIN

DEC CALIFORNIA CA 93
NOOTOON

SOFTWARE engineer Paul Mercer shares a jubilant moment with Capps and colleagues, from left, Greg Seitz and Michael Tibbott, after the first successful run of the software on the Newton hardware prototype. April 1992.

ment: "I finally decided that Xerox was never going to really move fast enough to get into this market."

Tesler's growing interest in personal computers brought him to Apple in 1980. The move was a significant change for him, since "it wasn't until Apple that I really got into doing products." One of his first projects was to work on the Lisa computer, a precursor to the Macintosh, released in 1983. Lisa was a $10,000, business-oriented desktop computer that failed in the marketplace despite its advanced technologies. It was just too expensive, and Apple ended up phasing it out for the sake of the Macintosh. After working on the Lisa, Tesler assumed several senior technology positions. By the time Sculley sent him to assess Newton, he was the company's vice president for advanced technology.

Tesler arrived at Newton's offices with a couple of basic assumptions: "We probably didn't want to do the product the group had in mind, and we just wanted to kind of take the technologies and the people and apply them to something that

used those technologies." It was unclear to the nervous engineers whether he would recommend saving the entire project, particularly given his close relationship with another in-house group, led by management consultant Marc Porat, that was competing directly with Newton. Following the announcement of Gassée's departure in March, the discouraged Newton engineers dropped everything. During this period, Capps and Jerome Coonen, a software manager, encouraged a last-ditch effort to revive interest in Newton. Their efforts paid off. Once the engineers had been roused from their initial depressed stupor, Capps noticed that "the group stopped doing anything except figuring out how to save the project."

The Newton team's lobbying effort began in earnest very quickly, on the night of March 11th, 1990, at a meeting Capps attended at Bill Atkinson's house to discuss formation of a new company that would include a loose team of engineers and managers working with Tesler and Porat on projects code-named Crystal and Paradigm. Atkinson had worked closely with

DAVE Murphy and fellow hardware engineers grapple with the complexities of infrared transmission, a unique feature that allows Newton machines to "beam" information back and forth to one another. April 1992.

SUSAN Schuman, Manager of Product Planning and Strategy Communications Products, during a meeting of the Newton product marketing group. She is responsible for developing and strengthening relationships with Apple's communications partners. April 1992.

company and meeting with executives, and concluded that Apple needed to move away from the Macintosh. Porat had Sculley's ear and was pushing the Crystal-Paradigm goal of developing a new interface for smart mobile telecommunications, a software standard called TeleScript that would allow for the free flow of information between most computing and communications devices. It seemed as though Apple was going to have to choose between Newton and Paradigm, and Capps knew that the Newton group's relative obscurity and Porat's politicking were both working against the recently abandoned researchers on Bubb Road.

Sculley was also at Atkinson's home that night. Capps was having fun showing off a $10,000 prototype of his newest invention, the Jaminator digiguitar, to the dozen or so assembled. While his colleagues took turns playing the Jaminator, Capps approached Sculley. "What's up with Newton, John?" **With nothing tangible but a simple, recycled slide show that the Newton group kept presenting during its few progress reports, it was easy to be dubious about the team's work.** Capps could see that Sculley was not exactly skeptical; in fact, he was interested in the project. But the boss's reply

Capps as an engineer on the Macintosh and was helping Porat develop his ideas about this new company. The Crystal-Paradigm folks were interested in developing technologies that paralleled some of Newton's work and had invited Capps to join the new venture.

Porat had been hired by his friend Tesler to explore new business directions Apple should pursue. He spent his year of employ rooting around the

"Apple is a really interesting place in terms of how it intro-duces a technology like this. You'd think that everyone in the company would be very receptive to new technologies, but because Apple is basically a one-brand company, there's so many fundamental questions about introducing a second brand. People get very nervous, and wonder, 'How close is it to Macintosh?' etc. because historically at Apple the new brand kills the old brand. Macintosh killed the Apple II. People have no model in their head of a multiple brand Apple. You go to these meetings and you have incredible arguments with people. The only people who really under-stand are people in the Newton group and people in our department. Everyone else in the company seems only to understand Newton as a new thing that would replace Macintosh—which is absolutely false. They should both be able to exist under the same umbrella." — Keith Yamashita

SOFTWARE Engineering Manager Donna Auguste, known by her childhood nickname Fi, leads a meeting of her software team. Auguste worked diligently to achieve cross-cultural representation among the group. April 1992.

0 1 : 3 7

was not encouraging: "I just don't understand it." Sculley was willing and wanting to understand it, particularly given the caliber of engineers working on the project and their belief in it, so he issued Capps a supportive challenge: The team had thirty days to create a Newton prototype to present to the board of directors, who were meeting in April.

Despite Sculley's liking of Newton and its vague fulfillment of his Knowledge Navigator product vision, he knew he would still have to prove its worth to an increasingly skeptical board. It was going to be a challenge. Sculley recognized "it was very difficult to get people within Apple to see the possibilities of where Newton could go." If the project was to survive, he and the Newton gang would have to fight the company's Macopic vision.

During the next few days, the Newton team mobilized. They decided to create a hardware prototype. Programmers and software engineers rarely produce such things, said Capps, and "never did any prototypes, but we actually went and hogged out a piece of plastic, put a display in it and ran an umbilical cord back to the Mac. It felt like a product." The crew then put together a digital show that would appear on the *faux*-Newton, driven by the Macintosh to which it was connected, with the desktop computer acting as a

smart, digital VCR to the prototyped Newton mini-video screen.

The engineers now had something tangible to present, but they wanted to go the extra mile to make sure they sold their project to Sculley and the board. To help them win this crucial battle, they hired a public relations specialist from Regis McKenna, a firm that had been consulting Apple since the company's early days. The consultant racked up her daily $1,000 fee and concluded: "You've got to hit Sculley with facts, facts, facts." Capps, speaking for the group, was not convinced. The discussion seesawed until he decided: "Listen, we've got to hit them with the emotional side first. Just grab them emotionally and then we can bring the facts and figures up."

Prior to the April board presentation, Capps showed Sculley the Newton prototype. While he was sequestered with the boss in a meeting room, some of his colleagues, their fate in the balance, waited and paced next door like expectant fathers in a maternity ward lounge. They had deliberately dimmed the lights in the conference room for dramatic effect. Capps thought the darkness of the chamber enveloped "this amazing, cool, backlit screen, and made the thing look golden. It was this magical thing." Capps stood there proudly holding the glowing, golden device. He handed it to Sculley. "Well, John,

TIM Parsey, right, in doorway with fellow designer Ray Riley, at the Apple Industrial Design Studio. Parsey and Riley were part of the team that came up with Newton's design in a two-week crash project with Sharp. The team also included Gavin Ivestor, Daniele Deluliis, Bob Brunner and Susanne Pierce. April 1992.

you've had a problem understanding what Newton was all about. Here's what we want to show you."

Sculley looked at the machine as it displayed some preprogrammed HyperCard stacks running simulations of functions he had always heard about, but was seeing now for the first time. The Newton simulated an architect's sketch pad and cleaned up the imprecise drawings, straightening lines and snapping them into symmetrical alignment. **Newton was no longer just a concept visualized by the mind's eye.** Now it was a prototype that fed Sculley's imagination. He looked up, inspired and relieved that he would not have to cancel the project. It clicked.

"Okay, I get it!"

Capps breathed a sigh of relief without dwelling on the victory and moved on to the slide show and some discussion, but the hard part was over. Sculley was enrolled.

The shock came immediately thereafter when Sculley handed the Newton team its new deadline: "Okay, two years from today." Capps thought Sculley's ultimatum was "like April Fool's or something." But that was not all. They still had to prove Newton's worth to the board. And the worst was to come. Capps' "technical brain was saying we couldn't do" what Sculley was demanding: "I want this product out and I want it to cost less than $1,500." The lowest price estimate they had reached at that point was $4,000, already half the cost of the original Newton.

Fifteen hundred dollars seemed impossible. So the Newton team, understanding the challenge and feeling the pressure, did what very ambitious, creative people do best: It agreed to meet the deadline and the price point.

· · · · ·

On April 18th, shortly after the successful board meeting, Tesler's technical review of Newton was officially announced. When he arrived, he found that he liked what he saw. "It was very easy to conclude very rapidly that it was a great concept. It just needed some modifications in terms of the hardware platforms."

Tesler realized that given the market pressure Apple was facing to license its Macintosh operating system and the ongoing search for ways to make its business less reliant on the roller coaster ride of hardware sales, Newton could move the company toward achieving one of Sculley's goals. Newton could be a way to develop a brand-new, non-Macintosh-based hard-

ware platform and operating system Apple could sell and broadly license. Tesler was happy that the Newton's long-term business proposition would fit into Sculley's plans, but it was mainly the developing technology itself that "toggled Tesler's bit," as Capps liked to say.

A new, still developing, high-level programming language, known by the code-name Ralph—named after Ralph Ellison, who wrote *The Invisible*

APPLE'S Director of Industrial Design, Bob Brunner, at right, models a hip-holster Newton accessory pouch for appreciative product designers Daniele Deluliis, center, and Johnathan Ive, far left. April 1992.

Man—was to be used, and there were plans to drive the machine with a new, highly efficient microprocessor. A new language, a new chip and a new machine; none of the technology would be off the shelf. **Newton would be many things, but above all, it would not be a personal computer.** It would be more than that. It was a research engineer's fantasy. An intrigued Tesler threw his support behind the group.

Tesler began leading the Newton team in May. Rejuvenated by Sculley's interest and the board's approval, the group's momentum faltered momentarily in July, when Apple announced it was spinning out Porat's group into a new company called General Magic, whose logo would be a rabbit being pulled out of a hat. The start-up received two of Apple's star software engineers, Atkinson and Andy Hertzfeld.

The Newton engineers were bewildered by the mixed signals they had received: support and endorsement from Sculley and the board on one hand and the formation of what they perceived to be direct competition on the other. Capps, whom General Magic was still pursuing, did not know whether "to go to General Magic or quit and go back to the Mac division or maybe just quit and join the Army."

In the end, he decided to stay with Newton, where he continued to work the long hours that would become a trademark for the group—a work ethic reminiscent of Apple's old Macintosh days, when product development was fueled by a sense of mission. The engineers got to work writing code, reviewing specifications for hardware and stripping out features. The long Newton days were broken up by informal basketball games held every afternoon next to the building. "No injuries" was the only rule the hackers respected during the sweaty, intense half-court matches. The style of play was at times as inventive as the code they wrote, though some of the more seasoned players were able to burn colleagues better than they burned code onto ROMs.

Thrashing on the blacktop is one thing; thrashing around for too long in the lab trying to reach decisions is another—engineers liked to call any protracted, convoluted selection process a "thrash." The former might hurt in the short run, but the indecision resulting from the latter can kill a project. Since the beginning of Newton's development, engineers had sought the perfect, energy-efficient microprocessor chip to run their final product. The chip was the nervous system of a product while the software did the thinking. The

PROGRAMMER Peter Alley rests during the big push prior to the Chicago Consumer Electronics Show. His trusty basketball and shoes, lower left, await him. April 1992.

named the AT&T chip "Hobbit." Although the Hobbit worked well for writing in C, it needed to be reworked for writing in Ralph, an incomplete language that few programmers working on Newton understood entirely.

Newton's consulting Ralph language specialists were less than thrilled with the Hobbit because they saw the chip as an added technical hurdle. Also, the Hobbit was not cheap, since, as Capps pointed out, AT&T was requesting a few million dollars to continue developing the chip, on top of the $1 million Apple had already spent on developing an earlier version. They were hooked on a chip that cost too much, needed too much adaptation and was causing too many headaches.

long process of selecting chips had caused major delays because the group looked at every processor on the market, as well as some that had never even made it there. They finally settled on a little-known AT&T product, the C Reduced Instruction Set Processor (CRISP), a chip suited to run code written in the "C" language (a popular language with which most programmers feel comfortable), although it would need some modification to fit the Ralph language Newton was using. Culbert, a J.R.R. Tolkien fan in his youth, code-

The search for the right chip continued, and precious days were wasted as discussions deteriorated into loud arguments. Tesler knew he had to resolve the microprocessor debate quickly so the engineers could stop treading water while they waited for a final chip design. On August 2nd, he sent Sculley an "eyes-only" memo informing him that his team could not take any more indecision over processors. By September 8, 1990, he had made a unilateral decision to replace AT&T's Hobbit with a new chip made by a small, overly acronymed British company, Advanced Reduced Instruction Set Chip (RISC) Machines, Limited, or ARM, Ltd. From then on, Tesler refused to look at any more processors. Case closed.

The Newton team now had a chip, a programming language, a mandate to proceed—and a fast-approaching deadline. The group of engineers, brimming with ideas about "cool and pure," latest and greatest technology, regularly lounged on couches that were not being used for sleeping, tossing back Pepsis and discussing how to solve technical challenges such as how to create collaborative mobile devices that used wireless communications. **The ideas were free-flowing and wide-ranging, and some of them had applications in the real world.** What the engineers lacked, Capps believed, was an understanding of the market for which they were developing a product. As a result, they had trouble focusing their work.

Capps was curious to find out how consumers functioned away from their desks. The "desktop metaphor" used for Macintosh computers was reflected in a screen filled with files, documents, calculators, folders and even a trash bin. The personal computer emulated a desktop. But what would Newton emulate? Early on, Capps had fired off a laundry list of questions to Apple's competitive analysis group: "What do people do with attaché cases? What do they do with dictating machines?" Capps was seeking more than an accounting of workers' needs away from their work stations and the ways Newton could meet them. He was "trying to find our center of gravity, our soul." For reasons unknown to him, he never received a reply.

With the Gassée-Sakoman regime gone, and its aversion to marketing types gone as well, Sculley insisted that Newton be assigned a marketing person. He recommended Michael Tchao. In June 1990, Tchao came to Newton after working on developments in multimedia, the type of technology that puts digitized mini-movies into personal computers. Prior to that, he had worked as a product manager with one of Apple's most criticized products, the Macintosh Portable. Tchao was glad to be joining Newton's distinguished team, but grew wary when he learned that the Newton product was supposed to be a "no-compromise" machine. That was the way the Macintosh Portable had been touted, as a "no-compromise" computer, but Tchao had found out the hard way that there would be a few compromises: size, weight and price. Introduced in September 1989, the sixteen-pound luggable, forty-megabyte, hard-drive machine with superior screen retailed at $6,499, plus tax. Perhaps it was no surprise that the Portable did not exactly fly off the shelves.

Tchao landed in the office next to Capps. Marketing and engineering were united for the first time in the Newton group, and sometimes the marriage caused embarrassment. Newton failed to recognize Tchao's handwriting, and Tchao asked Capps stinging questions: "What is the story with this recognition stuff? Is this going to work at all? Every time I try to write, it really sucks."

"Oh, don't worry, Michael, it'll get better. You've just got to sit down and train it. It'll learn."

Tchao hunkered down, trying to figure out what Newton was all about. Technically adept, he spent hundreds of hours with the engineers to see if he could work with them on solutions to marketing problems concerning the product's size and cost. Even with a $1,500 price tag, the thing was bound to be compared to a personal computer, especially since it was nearly as large as a laptop. Tchao noticed that not everyone was happy with the parameters into which they had been locked. He saw that "Capps especially was very frustrated" because the group was having trouble making progress.

The problem, Tchao believed, was that the Newton team was "juggling a lot of things." Alex Knight, another marketing specialist, hired by Tchao, joined Newton later that year and observed, "You can be cutting-edge on one or two things in a product, but you can't be cutting-edge on four core things—system architecture and communications architecture and the new language and the new processor—because those are going to come back and bite you."

Tchao struggled with marketing questions. "How are we going to reduce the risk and how can we get something out sooner? And how can we get something out cheaper? Can we have the best of all worlds, which is to get something out that's a first-generation product that gives us a holding place, knowing the corporate antibodies would not continue to fund us as we sorted this stuff out?"

Tchao and Capps spent days and nights talking things over in each others' offices. They finally decided that a smaller, cheaper, stripped-down version of Newton was the answer. Tchao knew the decision "was a compromise," a stopgap Newton that would not do everything a computer did, but still could be task-oriented with some communications functions. He sensed

MARGE Boots has designed a series of icons to help Newton users easily navigate through the product's various applications. Here, Boots points to the latest version she has created and solicits feedback from fellow team members. The icons have been revised again and again as a result of meetings like this one. April 1992.

"Interesting ideas," Tesler would sometimes agree, but the Capps-Tchao proposal would not be something the group would pursue. Decisions had already been made. A product was already being developed, even though it was a costly thing that was not easily handheld. No. No mini-Newton.

Tesler, who sometimes was called Mr. T, was not always a personable manager, although he was respected greatly for his technical genius. Whenever he returned to his office, he sat near a framed quote by the 19th-century German philosopher Arthur Schopenhauer, which he had propped up by his desk: **"Every truth passes through three stages before it is recognized. In the first it is ridiculed, in the second it is opposed, in the third it is regarded as self-evident."**

the need to get the machine into the market quickly so the company could buy time to improve the product and establish an early standard for devices with "intelligent assistance."

Furious ping-pong games went on in the Bubb warehouse's living room as Capps and Tchao hashed out ways to approach Tesler with their ideas. But the boss would not budge from his adherence to the original, larger Newton.

It was clear to Tchao and Capps that as far as the mini-Newton was concerned, Tesler was sitting squarely in Schopenhauer's second stage of truth recognition. They persisted through the fall and winter, frequently bringing up their ideas of how the first Newton product should look and be positioned, but Tesler opposed their plan. He was adamant. And he was the boss.

COPYWRITER Keith Yamashita, 25, pulls an "all-nighter" in the "BrainTank," the super-secret room at Apple where the Creative Services team he leads is developing the Newton logo, marketing materials and product packaging. April 1992.

t the beginning of 1991, Apple was enjoying increased revenues and rid-ing high on expectations in the stock market following successful sales of its new crop of low-cost Macintoshes, particularly the $999 Classic. Declaring a new product in a six-year-old Macintosh product line "classic" was just one indication of the accelerated and compressed time frame in which the technology was developing.

The larger Newton that Tesler favored took a back seat to the development of the Tchao-Capps handheld device following Tchao's meeting with Sculley on their February flight to Japan. Still, the shift was not immediate. Even though their idea had Sculley's approval, Tchao and Capps had yet to convince Tesler. Most creative decisions at Apple are not dictated or handed down from above, but require consensus. The engineer and the young marketing specialist lobbied Mr. T until the summer in subtle and surreptitious ways, and finally, indirectly, won him over. They convinced a Tesler ally within Newton to present him with their new, re-worked idea for Newton. The ploy worked. Tesler finally bought in to the proposal and his conversion moved the Capps and Tchao mini-model from "skunkworks" status to actual development. It became the first planned Newton product and was referred to as the

KEITH Yamashita checks with a courier service while supervising the creative services team as they prepare to show Newton packaging, store display and overall concept to buyers from the consumer electronics and office supply store chains. May 1992.

screen for hours on end while running tests or writing software and operating system code in a bizarre-looking language that demands an inordinate amount of punctuation, limits verb usage and appears grammatically convoluted when viewed as text. Engineers living and working in the virtual world behind a terminal screen and inside a compiling computer had to come up for air now and then. When they did, they drove down inside lanes or shot from outside the key of their nearby basketball court.

The hardware designers started working at the crack of dawn, while the software team hacked late into the night. Programmers spent most of 1991 indoors, their sun-unstroked faces illuminated by their VDT monitors' spectral radiation. **Their goal was to create a technology so smooth and seamless that, if successful, anyone using a Newton would be unaware that there was any technology involved at all.** The engineers would measure their success by the extent to which their work could be ignored in the end. The way Culbert figured it, "The goal of a good hardware platform is to be completely invisible—and it's very difficult to make hardware invisible. It's almost as difficult to make software transparent. If anything about the

"Junior." The original Newton "Senior" was still being developed, but its production would be put on hold until after Junior was born. The deadline was still mid-1992, less than a year away.

Everyone associated with the project was hard at work. There is little glamour in a job that requires one to sit in isolation, staring at a glowing

ART director, Andy Dreyfus examines the presentation materials and photos he and the Creative Services team have prepared for the next day's "channel suite" demos. May 1992.

hardware annoys the user, you're in trouble."

The group was not yet at a point where they had to worry about annoyed users. They were still busy dealing with their own frustration with Ralph, the untested, high-level language whose code name later was changed to Dylan—a name Apple trademarked and which ostensibly stands for "Dynamic Language." The split between those working on the Senior, with its seemingly boundless technologies and outstanding language problems, and the smaller, simpler Junior was quickly dividing the group. The "smirkers," who counted Capps among their number, were skeptical that the Senior product, running Dylan, could be made tolerably operable by product deadline. The conservatives, who included Tesler, faced a significant problem in that written Dylan-coded Newton features often took up too much of an already limited resource: space in random access memory (RAM). The less RAM space there was available, the more limited Newton's performance.

Dylan also was far from being perfected as a language. The process of running through instructions to execute certain functions was very slow because of the Dylan-inexperienced programmers' inability to find shortcuts or to write fluidly in it. The result was that Dylan's reflexes were retarded.

The smirkers felt that consumers had grown to expect electronic products that responded with lightning speed and that users would not tolerate waiting for seemingly interminable seconds to get Dylan's reaction. Though Dylan seemed likely to produce satisfactory results in the long run, the Newton engineers had little time now to refine it for their purposes.

During 1991, while the engineers attended to the task of designing hardware and software, management was slowly implementing Sculley's new business model by forging partnerships and licensing agreements. By September, following months of corporate courtship involving demonstrations and an expressed mutual desire to expand into undefined future markets, Apple entered formal negotiations with Sharp. The deal, to be sealed in half a year, was brokered by Hajime Ueda, a New York-based vice president for global project development at Nomura Research Institute, a Japanese consulting group. The agreement stipulated that the Japanese consumer electronics giant would manufacture Newton products for Apple and license the technology, so that nearly indistinguishable Newtons would eventually be

STEVE Capps hams it up while Michael Tchao runs through a dress rehearsal for the Newton product concept introduction at the Chicago Consumer Electronics Show. Capps and Tchao have developed a strong friendship and alliance through the process of creating Newton. May 1992.

sold by both companies in the same markets.

Sharp was a desirable partner for Apple and the Newton product because of its flat-screen technology, experience in microelectronics manufacturing and understanding of the extant electronic organizer market, which was dominated by its Wizard products. The relationship between Apple and Sharp was able to blossom despite the Japanese company's initial reservations that Apple would encroach on its organizer market with a Newton product that positioned itself somewhere between a Wizard and a personal computer. A successful Newton would clearly put the future of the Wizard in jeopardy.

. . . . .

The new year rang in with dramatic changes throughout the world. The Soviet Union had just put itself out of business and the global economy was quickly reconfiguring, but time seemed frozen back in Cupertino, where Newton engineers still hunched silently over their keyboards. Hack, hack, hoops, hack. 1992 arrived and the engineers continued their single-minded pursuit: creating Newton's body and soul.

The smirkers clashed one final time with the grin-and-bear-it Senior and Dylan loyalists in a showdown at an off-site meeting in January 1992, a meeting Tesler called to end the Junior-Senior riff and the language debate once and for all. In keeping with the team's cloistered existence, the gathering took place at a Catholic retreat on the San Francisco peninsula. Surrounded by icons of California Christianity—Jesus in batik and a depiction of the Last Supper in seashells—the smirkers resurrected their concerns about

KEITH Yamashita, right background, and Andy Dreyfus, left background, labored around the clock with their Creative Services team to create store-display and packaging materials for Newton. A seasoned buyer for the Staples office supply chain, center, looks at the store display and remarks, "It doesn't get any better than this!" May 1992.

Dylan and set off a heated argument that culminated with an authoritative yet paternal Tesler saying, "There's a lot of trade-offs that we have to make, but this is not one of them. This decision will not be changed." Tesler's research roots drew him viscerally to the challenge and beauty of both the larger Senior jam-packed device and Dylan's theoretical possibilities. He seemed not to be able to see the larger product's problems and the language's more limited, actual capabilities. Dylan, he pronounced in superior tones, was there to stay.

Markets, however, were changing. Sculley defined the development of a personal digital assistant (PDA) market and staked out Apple's leadership role in that market by both announcing the category and his intention to develop a PDA product during a wide-ranging speech at the Consumer Electronics Show (CES) held the same month in Las Vegas. The public coming-out party for Junior, though not public knowledge, was scheduled for the next CES, to be held in Chicago that May.

The Chicago CES was the traditional show for products planned for sale in the lucrative Christmas market—in which Apple's personal computers sell best, along with the late-spring graduation sales period.

Sculley was taking a huge risk by announcing a prototype at a show where everyone else was announcing actual products. If he had no product to sell by Christmas, then of course none would be sold—and Apple's reputation would suffer because of Sculley's unkept promise.

Having such an accelerated schedule for market delivery meant that Newton had to be presentable for the May CES and be shipping shortly thereafter. The product also had to have a public image as strong as the new bond created between Newton's marketing and engineering teams. Part of that image would result from the work of Apple's Industrial Design group. Another part would come from the findings of the new User Experience group, which Tesler had formed to analyze people's interaction with Newton.

The most public of images, the advertising, point-of-purchase displays, logos, videos, packaging—nearly everything that would define Newton in the public eye—required the services of a creative team. Tchao went to Apple's in-house Creative Services division to find Newton's image-makers. A few members of the division, including Keith Yamashita, a young copywriter originally hired by Apple who had just returned from Jobs' post-Apple venture,

NeXT, met with Tchao and listened to his spiel: "We're going to CES and our intent there is to launch Newton to the world. Would you guys like to help?" Some tentative nods brought Tchao to a more important point: "There are some ground rules. **Newton is so fundamentally different from anything Apple has ever done, you're really going to have to divorce yourself from everything you know about Macintosh, what Apple's about, all the rules you know and the way we've done business in the past.** You're going to have to take a very, very fresh approach to doing this." Tchao had struck a nerve. Yamashita was inspired and signed up immediately.

By January, Yamashita had launched the "BrainTank." A windowless, white room with tables and chairs, about the size of two side-by-side squash courts, the BrainTank became a round-the-clock idea chop-shop where Newton's identity would be created. The secret room was open only to Newton team members, whom Tchao pushed to communicate with one another "because we really want everything to be integrated. We're asking the engineering teams, the human interface teams, the product design teams, the marketing teams, all to work together concurrently because we want to get

this product to market quickly and we want everything unified." According to Tchao, while the BrainTank was perhaps not the first integral concept unit in U.S. marketing and product identity history, what was created there was done in record time. It was certainly the first time in Apple history. Anyone walking into the room could hear that it hummed.

Almost overnight, the chamber was filled with the churnings of creative

JOHN Sculley makes a point to Michael Tchao during a dress rehearsal for their presentation at the CES in Chicago. May 1992.

JEAN Stevens of creative services takes a beer break. It's 9:30 p.m. in the "channel suite"— and the Newton team is far from ready for next morning's demos. Promotional materials have just arrived from the printer and Stevens and Greta Mikkelsen, at left, will work into the wee hours preparing the room. May 1992.

2 0

STEVE Capps answers Sharp executives' questions during an informal meeting the night before the CES presentation in Chicago. May 1992.

RENÉE Adomshick has been organizing the chaos for the Newton team for the last two years in her role as Area Associate to Michael Tchao. In a meeting the night before the product concept introduction at CES she appeared to be the only calm person in the room. May 1992.

"I remember very well the early, early days in one of our brainstorming sessions. We were all sitting around asking, 'Who do we want to build this product for?' And people were saying, 'I just want my mother to have one of these things and be able to write a letter to me and say, Hi, John, I'm fine. Signed Mom—without having to read a page of instructions—and then just print it or send it off.'"

— SHIFTEH KARIMI

staff. Yamashita understood the BrainTank to be "a place where everything would be confidential, would always be locked up, but all team members from all sides could come and really think about the product: How will people understand it? How should we build the brand? How should we explain it to people?" The walls were plastered from floor to ceiling with different-sized concept and story boards. **Newton clearly showed that it was parting with Apple tradition in every possible way, beginning with something as small as typeface.** Multicolor posters were printed in the more angular Gil Sans Light, a font distinctly not the Apple Garamond used for nearly every document ever previously published by the company.

Late one night, Tchao brought Capps over to the BrainTank. Capps was excited to see the first glimpses of how Newton would look outside the seclusion of Apple's walls. He was impressed to find the creative team hanging around the engineers, asking questions and gauging expectations, before returning to their work-space to come up with the exact, right way to represent Newton. During this 2:00 a.m. visit, Capps pulled out a one-dollar bill and fastened it above the doorway. Yamashita understood what the gesture

meant. "It was to symbolize the trust; he was going to leave all his money and everything entrusted to this room."

Working in tandem with the BrainTank on Newton's public presentation was Tim Parsey's Industrial Design team, housed in a separate warehouse. Parsey had designed U.S. Olympic team sleds, ski watches, medical braces and rental-car company computers before joining Apple, where he was responsible for redesigning Newton's housing during the run-up to CES. The Newton assignment made for "a two-week crunch project" with his California team, which exchanged ideas with Sharp's designers in Japan. Parsey's goal was "to create something that has a simple power" and his team worked hard to refine Newton's form. With the Sharp designers, they came up with an initial Junior design featuring a double-hinged lid that flipped open over the back and was meant to be held like a stenographer's notebook. Test users noted that a couple of rubber-tipped pads on which the closed lid rested reminded them of breasts. The design team scrapped the lid.

Shifteh Karimi, an educational psychologist who led Newton's user-testing program, was also trying to find out how to bring the best-looking and best-working product to the public. She suggested that Newtons be given to a

STEVE Capps and other software programmers work at 2:00 a.m. to debug the demonstration they developed for John Sculley's presentation, scheduled to begin at 10:00 that morning. The demo continues to crash, so the team works through the night to get the job done. May 1992.

WALTER Smith, left, and Steve Capps spend the night prior to the Newton technology introduction debugging the product. May 1992.

ULTRA Man spins in a Chicago hotel room where Newton programmers debug through the night. May 1992.

IN Chicago for the CES, Sharp executives, left to right, Masafumi Morimoto, Division Deputy General Manager, Dr. Atsushi Asada, Senior Executive Vice President, and Akira Mitarai, Corporate Director—partners with Apple in the creation of Newton—arrive at Park West, the nightclub where Apple will announce its new technology. Sharp will manufacture the Newton and has licensed the technology from Apple to create its own version of the product, which will be sold in the same market. May 1992.

JOHN Sculley checks the morning story about Newton in *USA Today* on his way to a live interview on *CBS This Morning* prior to the product concept introduction in Chicago at CES. With him, from left, are Daniel Paul, Apple's Hollywood liaison, Gabi Schindler of Regis McKenna, and Brooke Cohan from Apple public relations. May 1992.

group of testers whose reactions could be noted by engineering and marketing. Tesler had understood the importance of watching the way users interact with new products and technologies since his early days working on the Lisa computer, when he gained new engineering ideas from such observations. For Newton, Tesler put Karimi in charge of the new, interdisciplinary "User Experience" team of engineers and psychologists. She invited volunteer users with little knowledge of the machine to try mocked-up software and features while their experience was videotaped. These studies helped the engineers modify functions including the system for filing information on Newton's screen, which felt right in the lab but odd to the non-technical user.

Overtime was not in the team's vocabulary since everyone was working toward the same goal during the next few months' race toward the Chicago CES's May deadline. **The BrainTank bubbled while engineering shifted away from its work on the product to concentrate on building a working prototype to present to the press.** Sleep became a distant memory as low-grade hysteria from overwork and overextension increased.

. . . . .

When Newton team members walked into Chicago's cavernous CES exhibition center just off Lake Michigan, they were overwhelmed by blaring, big-screen TVs and Top Forty tunes shrieking from hundreds of car stereos. Slick salesmen were energetically extolling the virtues of their equipment to buyers from major retail chains and electronics stores, who were as streetwise as they were aware of profit margins. To a CES newcomer, the show

JOHN Sculley and public relations aide Gabi Schindler share a limo ride following a 5:00 a.m. interview on *CBS This Morning*. They are heading to a dress rehearsal at the nightclub where the Newton product concept presentation will begin at 10:00 a.m. May 1992.

0 1 : 1 2

STEVE Capps and his colleagues are able to grab fifteen minutes of sleep after delivering the debugged Newton presentation to the Chicago nightclub where John Sculley is about to introduce Newton technology. May 1992.

1   1

might appear filled with a multitude of fast-talking men whose teeth seemed sharper and sales instincts keener than those of ordinary mortals—the result, perhaps, of an evolutionary process of survival in the highly competitive consumer marketplace. One thing was clear, and that was Apple was no longer in the New Age world of Macworld computer shows, where granola-bar-crunching exhibitors still distributed "shareware" at disk-duplication cost. Here, the company was competing for attention in a hot-dog-chomping crowd full of commissioned salespeople looking to close a quick deal and make quota on items like remote control units that retailed for $19.95.

Traditionally, computers are introduced at computer shows. CES in 1992 was primarily a venue for the consumer electronics industry to check out the latest VCR and CD technology and products, and Apple's presence was a bit of an anomaly. **But Sculley predicted a convergence of markets as well as industries, and he sensed that the distinction between consumer and business markets was blurring.** Computer technology was finding its way into more consumer hands as the price of hardware dropped and its applications expanded to accommodate consumer needs. Newton's introduction at CES was yet another indication that this would be no ordinary computer.

Yamashita and the rest of the BrainTankers arrived in Chicago and set up a "channel suite" in the Park Hyatt Hotel, a room in which buyers from the consumer electronics "channels" could view Newton materials. Yamashita unloaded boxes filled with information and accouterments they had worked on nonstop since the BrainTank started, including a point-of-purchase display, four videos, posters, brochures and product packaging. He prepared for the arrival of potential channel partners from major nationwide chains, who had been invited to a special Newton preview that would take place prior to the CES press demonstration the following day.

Yamashita's goal at CES was to identify gaps in the forthcoming Newton campaign, "to start getting feedback on how to sell it, how to price it, what's the brand, what's the name, how do you display it." The Brain-Tank's work had been fast and furious, and the Tankers had tried to have fun, but they had also been working far from the real world in a locked room in Cupertino. Until Chicago, their only outside feedback had come from paid visiting consultants who had tried to give Newton a new, consumer-friendly

STEVE Capps has slept only a couple of hours during the last several days, but still manages to deftly answer questions from enthusiastic reporters who've surrounded him following the Newton product concept introduction at the Chicago CES. May 1992.

name. In the name game, Tchao preferred simplicity over flash, which is why he agreed with Yamashita "not to choose 'ZippyPad' or 'BrainAmplifier' or 'PowerEnabler.'" The consultants had hundreds of names including "KnowPad" and "MessagePad with Intelligence by Newton." So far, none of the names had stuck.

When a group of buyers representing various outlets came to the channel suite, Yamashita showed them a video and briefed them about Newton. The group then moved to another room in the suite where they saw the

posters, packaging and point-of-purchase display—a novelty in Apple's marketing history. Such elaborate displays were common for consumer goods, but a point-of-purchase display in a computer store is very simple: the computer itself, either switched on or off, running third-party software. When a gruff, tough minded buyer from the office supply chain Staples began examining the Newton's point-of-purchase display, Yamashita approached him nervously. "What do you think?"

The buyer squinted at Yamashita, assessing the kid for what seemed like an eternity. Finally, a smile crossed his face. "It doesn't get any better than this," he barked. Yamashita was surprised. What did the man think when he compared the point-of-purchase display to Sharp's materials? The buyer laughed. "No one has anything that compares to this. Not Sharp or anyone."

Yamashita was elated. **The positive feedback kept coming from one buyer after another. Stunned and very happy, the BrainTank crew knew it had won Chicago's first Newton team victory.** At the very least, Apple would have a shot at selling Newton through non-traditional computer channels. Now it was up to the machine to live up to its image.

SOFTWARE engineer Andy Stadler stands at the podium where Sculley has just finished his Newton presentation. May 1992.

01 : 08

"One of the major areas of development was a whole new programming language being created in parallel with hardware and other parts of the software. It was code-named Ralph. And I had my job cut out for me—just inheriting a product code-named Ralph was a challenge right off the bat. And an even bigger challenge was this technology which was basically just getting developed, just getting designed, in parallel with a huge platform effort. So you can imagine the risk. You sort of quadruple your risk when you build a new paradigm and a new computing environment on top of a whole new language technology." — JAMES JOAQUIN

In Suite 316, one floor down from the channel display room, Capps and the other engineers set up a "bug-squashing tank." The prototype that Sculley would be presenting the next morning was far from perfect; system errors kept appearing and causing the machine to crash at the most inopportune moments, as when they botched a demonstration for already-skeptical Sharp representatives the night before.

The work seemed endless. The engineers began tag-team debugging and coding. One exhausted engineer slept while another pushed himself to his limit. Then they traded places. Operators changed, but the coding was constant. The suite took on the flavor of a dorm room just before final exams. One of the engineers suspended a mascot from the ceiling, a battery-powered plastic Ultra Man cartoon character that whirled around the room in wide arcs at eye level. The toy spun around and conked anyone entering the room right in the head. Otherwise, the room was notable for the smell of pizza and a preponderance of empty soda cans.

The second day and night of nonstop debugging was driving the engineers a little mad, and some of their temporary insanity and invective found its way into the crevices of code that can hold non-instructional language. **Profanity was dropped in, not to affect the machine's performance but to express the writers' frame of mind.** Scream of consciousness hacking.

Sculley arrived in Chicago in the midst of the debugging marathon to run through a presentation rehearsal that was divided in two parts. The development of QuickTime, an Apple software package that made computers into moving image players, and the digital compression tools of multimedia that allowed for sound, text and visuals to coalesce would be Sculley's opening act; PDAs and Newton the closer. By 6:00 a.m. on May 29, 1992, Sculley was sitting in a limousine, reading an article about Apple in *USA Today* and cruising to a *CBS This Morning* interview at the CES exhibition halls. With him was a Newton prototype to flash for the cameras, a machine that was difficult

KEITH Yamashita celebrates with the Newton team after a successful introduction of Newton technology. May 1992.

0 6

to hold for more than five or ten minutes because, due to an unresolved power supply problem, it would get burning hot when its tightly packed electronic components went about nearly audibly sucking dry the battery pack.

Inside the rented nightclub where Apple was going to make its presentation, Capps and some of the other engineers were beyond exhaustion and had fallen asleep on banquettes near the stage. **Four-and-a-half years of effort and the countdown work of countless sleepless nights in the run-up to Chicago were going to be judged on the basis of a ninety-minute show with a prototype. If the demonstration and prototype did not work now, there was nothing they could do about it.**

By 9:45 a.m., a perturbed press corps had been waiting too long outside the doors of the rented nightclub. Inside, the public address system boomed, "Fifteen minutes to showtime, people." Capps hopped up and looked alive. Shortly, he would be on stage using his handwriting to show how, and if, Newton worked.

Roughly 600 journalists shoved their way in and competed for the

available seats, realizing that many would be left standing. Sculley took the stage and, standing alone in front of a blue curtain framed by four giant screens, started his speech. The day before, he had decided to change his presentation dramatically. Instead of concentrating on multimedia and compression, he wanted to make it Newton's day. He chucked a good portion of the previous script and went straight for the jugular, introducing Tchao and emphasizing that Newton "is not just about a product or even a technology. It is about nothing less than a revolution." Sculley then turned the floor over to Tchao with a stage whisper: "Let's hope it works."

As Sculley was speaking, an unfamiliar man showed up at the nightclub entrance and requested to be let in. He was told no, since he was not on the guest list. He then pleaded, "Could I at least have a press kit?" The woman monitoring the door looked at him querulously. "Well, no, there are only enough press kits for invited guests. We don't have any extra ones to give out. We can give you a copy of the press release, maybe, but not the press kit." "But I'm a friend of Michael Tchao's." "Okay, I'll go check."

Just as he was about to go on stage, Tchao was told that someone was asking for publicity material. Tchao suspected that the man was trying to get information for Microsoft. Give him a press kit? "No, definitely not!"

The presentation went on as events at the distant entrance went unnoticed. The door monitor came back and told the interloper, "I'm sorry, but I can't give you a press kit." The man sighed and walked out dejectedly, only to come storming back into the room seconds later and grab one of two unclaimed press kits still sitting on the table just inside the door. He rushed out to his waiting car with the loot. A beefy bouncer who came as part of a package deal with the rented nightclub jumped up. "Hey, was he supposed to have that?" "No!" the woman at the door shouted.

The muscle man ran after the press kit-napper and wrestled away the pictures and papers. Defeated, the man dove into the back seat of his chauffeur-driven car and slammed the door. The car squealed away, as Brooke Cohan and security guards watched dumbfounded.

Tchao finally took the stage. He held aloft a battery-powered Newton prototype and told the audience that he was there to show that it was real and it worked. The demonstration they were about to see, he noted, was running on real Newton hardware and software. **Tchao flipped the switch and . . . nothing.** Quickly, he put the machine away and moved on to his speech about Newton's ability to capture, organize and communicate bits and pieces of information exchanged and gathered in modern daily life—phone numbers, business cards, notes, appointments. It was a smart product that could actually phone and fax people after receiving written messages as simple as "Call Bob." "Capture, organize and communicate" was the distilled party line, the Newton "message" that would be repeated endlessly.

Coming off his first flop in which Newton had done nothing, an embarrassed Tchao initially stumbled on his words. The lights and the pressure were intense, and it was hard to gauge the audience's level of interest. He introduced Capps, who was on stage to perform a demonstration "by a real engineer." A real tired engineer.

Capps, facing a sea of suits while attired in his habitual shorts, open-collared shirt and Vans, began to bang through a demonstration using a Newton that was hooked up to a Macintosh hosting the Newton hardware and software used in the demo. He showed a way to order pizza by moving icons of toppings onto a graphically represented pie and then faxing the order by pointing the stylus at a "fax" command. "Ooohs" and "aaahs" from the audience.

Capps then used the stylus to write "Call Michael" on the screen. The display verified his command. The room filled with the sound of seven electronic phone beeps coming from the amplified Newton speaker. Capps ran through the demonstration as if it were the easiest thing he had ever done. It was fluid. It was fast. There was barely enough time for journalists to jot down notes on all the functions since Capps moved from one to the next without pause. Witnessing successful handwriting recognition captivated more than a few spectators. It was a phenomenal display, even by Apple's standards.

Phoning, faxing, freestyle writing. **Newton had succeeded not only in completing all of these technical tasks, but also in impressing the hell out of the assembled press, many of whom had expected yet another speech full of Sculley's vision and far-off product plans.** What they got instead was a look at a technology on which Apple was basing its future and a product that would define a new market. The PDA market.

In an act of redemption at the end of the presentation, Tchao returned to the stage and held up a prototype to prove that the unattached, battery-powered Newton was real, as he had claimed earlier, and that it could in fact

MICHAEL Tchao dances into the early morning hours at Blue Chicago, a popular Windy City bar. He has spent the last several years working to make Newton a reality, and after the successful presentation he, John Sculley and others made at CES, he is one step closer to his dream. May 1992.

work. His first attempt had been subverted, he realized, because the unit had no power. Sculley had been asked to leave the same unit on during his television interview earlier that morning and the batteries had gone dead. During Capps' demonstration of the podium-tethered Newton, Culbert, who suspected a power problem, replaced Tchao's handheld unit's four AAA battery cells backstage. Those batteries would keep the Newton prototype alive for only about twenty minutes.

After Tchao's concluding demonstration, press photographers rushed

the stage. They wanted a shot of Newton, a shot at holding it. After an hour-and-a-half of showmanship and technological razzle-dazzle, Newton went from a public rumor to an expected product. Now, all the Newton team had to do was create the real thing.

Most of the Appleniks who achieved success in Chicago that day were young; their success was heady. It meant that they would be noticed by people both within and outside the company. **They were kids who seemed to be having a good time playing around in the grown-up world.** However, soon they would be seeing their product group fitting into Apple's larger corporate structure. Shortly, the team would lose some of its treasured independence. But they did not know that yet.

The work ahead would be ever more demanding, but Newton's clear moment of success in its first public outing called for celebration. Tesler toasted his engineers at dinner before the rest of the gang descended on the Blue Chicago blues club, where drinking and dancing were unrestrained. Capps was the only team member who missed the party. He was back at the hotel, fast asleep.

FRAM BLOOZ

Well I've been hacking all night,
We still haven't got to Alpha.

Well my monitor she glows so bright,
At least she's not filled up with Ralph-a.

'Cause I got the FRAM Blues,
And I don't know when it will get through.

I'm watching day turn into night,
I can't get my code to work just right.

Everybody's home sick with the flu,
Lord knows my frames are giving me the blues.

Night's getting blacker by the hour,
Those gum balls sure are mighty sour.

I got the FRAM blues,
Just don't know when it will get through.

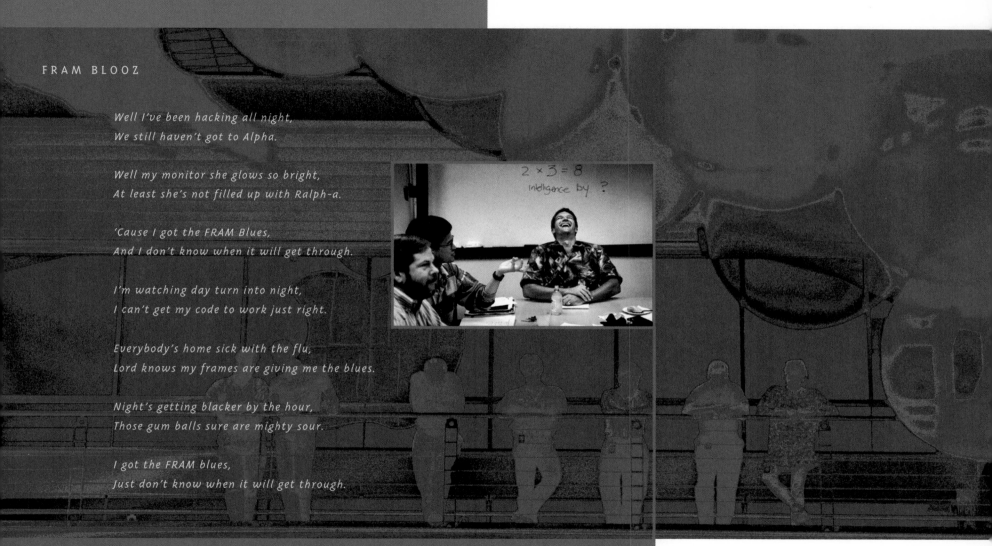

2 × 3 = 8
intelligence by ?

MARKETING Director Burt Cummings reacts to an ironic comment by Michael Tchao, at left, during a meeting of the Newton marketing team. After months of unrelenting pressure, humor is warmly welcomed by the group. On the board is a reference to the powerful math capability planned for the first Newton product. The feature was later abandoned when its lead programmer went on maternity leave before she could finish it. With the rest of the programming team already putting in eighty-hour weeks, no one could spare the time to take on even one more project. August 1992.

E ngineers liked to joke that the development paradigm in the computer industry always had been 1) print the T-shirt, 2) design the icon, 3) develop the product. Now it could include 4) write the song.

With deadlines now memories and work that remained undone, the Newton team was singing the blues. Music and lyrics were written by Capps and company and performed by programmers Walter Smith, a.k.a. "Dr.

Ralph," on guitar, Capps on bass, Martin Gannholm on vocals and a reticent Ko Isono on a makeshift tambourine made from a cupful of pushpins. One of the musicians also played a Jaminator, the guitar Capps had invented a few years earlier that produced perfect riffs every time. He had recently licensed it to a Japanese toy company to manufacture and distribute.

The engineering team had good reason to sing the blues. Following Newton's success at the Chicago CES, where Apple had announced partnerships with Sharp, Motorola, PacTel, Random House and others, it became obvious to everyone watching that Newton was real—at least real enough to jolt competing companies into proclaiming that they, too, were creating PDAs. **Newton was no longer alone.** CES also brought the Newton product group to the attention of those within corporate Apple who had either ignored or begrudged the project in the past. Many now wanted either a piece of the hot action or resented the increasing percentage of company resources Newton required, especially since it would not generate any immediate revenue. It also became obvious to Newton group members that their deadline to ship the product would slip, partly because of their difficulty in developing Dylan, a language they started to abandon a week after

HARDWARE engineers test a new version of the ARM RISC chip in the Newton lab.

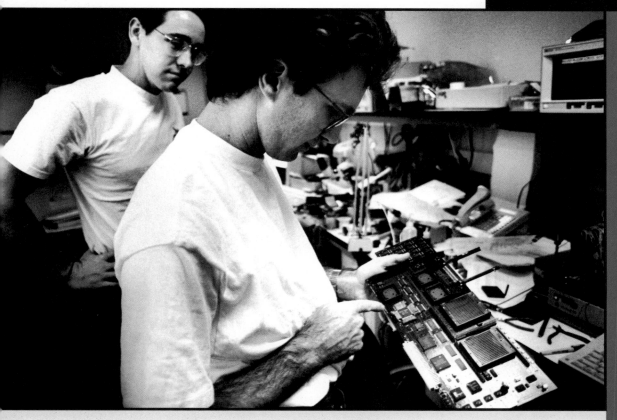

"When we started the PIE Division, we talked about building a new business model for Apple, given the dynamics of the computer industry—that it was starting to mature, which translated into potential decreases in margins for Apple. So we had to look at new business models, and part of the reason for setting up the Personal Interactive Electronics Division was obviously to enter into the consumer marketplace. But, in addition to that, we needed to build a new business model that would make economic sense in these smaller margin businesses. So what we want to do, besides developing the great technology that we keep developing at Apple, is build a strategy where we could start licensing and potentially OEMing that technology to other companies. This way we could help build a very broad base of customers for our products and help establish a *de facto* market standard because we were able to get product in the marketplace fairly quickly."

— BARRY SCHIFFMAN

"The product itself needs to be tough and rugged, but at the same time very sophisticated, creating a new stake in the ground for Apple and therefore having a strength about its design—a recognizability." — TIM PARSEY

CES, along with the Newton Senior product—despite Tesler's emphatic declaration that Dylan was the chosen language at the off-site meeting six months earlier.

As they crawled toward the fall, Tesler finally lost his battle to keep Senior and Dylan alive. He had sacrificed most of his well-deserved summer sabbatical in a futile attempt to make his project work. Locking himself in a conference room with a few staunch allies in June, Tesler went to work and hacked for four weeks straight. Health considerations were put on hold as he sat in front of the computer tapping away at the keyboard for endless hours, wearing wrist supports because of metacarpal problems. To make sure that the work went uninterrupted, Tesler's secretary, Mary Reagan, informed callers that he was still on leave even though he was only steps away inside the building.

Despite Tesler's concerted efforts, the language still caused the machine to go clunk. **By the time fall arrived, Dylan had departed. The Newton team would now sing its software blues exclusively in the key of "C."** Ironically, the AT&T's Hobbit chip, suited perfectly for C, was long gone. The ARM 610 microprocessor continued to be used in the one remaining Newton product,

the Junior. Changing the language meant throwing away much of the already developed code, and abandoning Senior meant junking many of the technologies that would have been included in the larger product. Larry Kenyon, who started at Apple in 1980 and was an original Newton team member who later became a software manager for Newton, compared the language switch to the team's earlier decision to change the processing chip, which he

SOFTWARE engineer Scott Zimmerman, 33, exhausted and resting in his Paris hotel room after flying in from the Newton lab in Cupertino, California, to help demonstrate Newton to the European press. September 1992.

JAMES Joaquin pretends he is Apple President Michael Spindler during a dress rehearsal for a Newton demonstration to the European press. September 1992.

JAMES Joaquin makes a call to the States as Scott Zimmerman checks out French TV while holed up in the Hotel Le Meridien during their visit to Paris to demonstrate Newton at the Apple Expo. September 1992.

FROM left, David Seda, Raymond Nasr and Jean Luc Lebrun, seated, listen to Apple President Michael Spindler during a rehearsal for an Apple new products presentation at the Apple Expo in Paris. Although the Newton demonstration lasted for just five minutes, the machine received significantly more coverage in the French press than other Apple products. September 1992.

0 0 : 9 3

"There's a trend throughout the world, and now it's coming to the U.S., to do much faster product development. One way to do so is by putting together teams that have individuals from different function groups that work together as a product team. We just are off making this product happen. And this team may dissolve once this product is out, or it may reformulate into a different combination of people to do other products." — PHIL BAKER

MICHAEL Spindler makes a humorous entrance at the beginning of his presentation to the European press at the Apple Expo in Paris. Wearing the DynaMac, a prototype of a virtual reality Macintosh developed several years earlier, Spindler hoped to drive home his belief that technology concepts are becoming reality at a breakneck pace. September 1992.

NEWTON developer relations expert James Joaquin gets made-up before going on stage in Paris to demonstrate Newton to the European press. Joaquin owns part of Extra Large, a hip-hop clothing company, and spends his spare time rapping with a San Francisco band. September 1992.

JAMES Joaquin shows Newton up close to members of the European press. September 1992.

JAMES Joaquin relaxes in a Parisian taxi and reflects on the flawless Newton demo he just performed with Apple President Michael Spindler for the European press. September 1992.

0 0 : 8 9

estimated "probably threw us off by a year or so. Because you don't want to change. You need to focus to get a product out."

A commitment that goes well beyond simple focus and diligence is required to write more than one million lines of code, scrap much of it and then continue to hack away toward the 750,000 lines that the Junior product would eventually need to function. Sometimes, in the heat of compiling, Capps would consider the task at hand and find himself genuinely amazed. "There's just never been something that has this many lines of code and has been done this hectically that any of us know about." Newton's 750,000 lines of code equaled the sum written for the Macintosh, the Macintosh Plus, the Macintosh II and a few other Apple machines to boot. Capps recognized the team's quick achievement was all the more extraordinary because the codes for each of those other machines "were all written over the course of four or five years. It's amazing it works at all."

Writing thousands of lines of new code on insane deadlines was hard enough, but the pressure on the Newton team was worsened because the competition was heating up. It was clear that Apple, as a leading-edge technology company, was setting its sights on an undeveloped market from which others could profit. AT&T saw the potential early on and, according to Capps, gave away its Hobbit chip to GO, a company based in Mountain View, California, that was working on a notebook-sized, pen-based, writing-tablet-shaped computer with extended communications capabilities and a built-in hard drive. Capps saw the irony in GO's using Hobbit: "Our code name has become the basis of this chip. They didn't even have the dignity to change it."

JAMES Joaquin, center left, talks about Newton to members of the European press who've just seen his demonstration of the technology at the Apple Expo in Paris. Engineer Scott Zimmerman, packing up his equipment, is eager to trek to the nearby McDonald's he scoped out earlier in the trip. For Zimmerman, a day without his ration of five cheeseburgers is like a day without croissants for a native Parisian. September 1992.

PRODUCT Marketing Specialist Joyce Gelbach beats James Joaquin, right, at Foosball during a break from their daylong meeting with Apple Europe employees in Paris. October 1992.

"What's very interesting about the Newton team is they are renegades. Their philosophy is, 'It's better to do it and try it, see how it works, and apologize to folks later.' The rest of Apple right now is in this analytical mode where they want to know all the answers, and with a technology like this it's virtually impossible to know. Someone needs to make an educated choice and go for it." — KEITH YAMASHITA

KEITH Yamashita reflects on the many new problems facing the Newton team while riding the Paris Metro on his way to help demonstrate Newton to Apple's European employees. October 1992.

At around the same time, Casio, which had already released a digital organizer product called B.O.S.S., decided to join with Tandy to announce the development of a Newton clone they would call the Zoomer. But the most serious threat to Apple's gambit arose from rumors that Microsoft had put together a development team working on a "Newton-killer." The Seattle company was aiming to create a product called the WinPad. General Magic, that less than cooperative coopetitor, also loomed in the background, as the word

swirled through Silicon Valley that it was planning to manufacture a specific product and not just develop communications software technology. The stakes were suddenly much higher than anyone had expected before CES.

The corporate need to limit risk was rising as well. Later that summer, a reconfiguration of Apple incorporated the Newton product group into a larger functional group called Personal Interactive Electronics (PIE). In addition to overseeing Newton, the Apple PIE encompassed multimedia, interactive CDs, voice recognition and on-line services. It published software and other media titles and developed new, consumer-oriented technologies that were still being investigated.

The structural reorganization was complete by the fall of 1992 and effectively stripped away some responsibilities from Newton's marketing managers. **It also added extra strain on the engineers, who not only were under the gun to finish writing code, but also had to take time now to explain what they were doing to new PIE colleagues and to engineers who were no longer hacking for the now-defunct Senior product.** They also had to take time to demonstrate

BURT Cummings "goes off-line" with a member of the Newton product marketing team during a break from a sometimes heated meeting with Apple Europe employees. The Europeans expressed frustration with the lag time in getting information about Newton, but with the project moving so fast there was little Cummings could do. September 1992.

KEITH Yamashita, James Joaquin and Michael Tchao listen to Joyce Gelbach as they wait to make presentations to Apple Europe employees at the company's Paris office. October 1992.

technologies to potential licensees and adjust to new managers. Tesler was understated when he called his job "an impossible management challenge."

The Newton marketing division's Knight described the turn of events by quoting from the *Gilligan's Island* theme song: CES went so smoothly for the Newton team, he said, "It started out as a three-hour cruise." But immediately afterwards, "The weather started getting rough, the tiny ship was tossed."

The PIE-directed Newton team may have felt as though they were lost at sea, but Apple as a whole was feeling temporarily buoyed by a spurt in revenues caused by the recently released Macintosh PowerBook, a product that would garner over $1 billion in first-year sales and become the best selling laptop in the market. Dramatic sales and increasing market share came at a time of concurrently diminishing profits, however, and Apple products were forced to react to a personal computer market trend of constantly dropping retail prices. The downward pressure on profits presented an impending problem for a company still addicted to high double-digit profit margins that once ran well above 50 percent.

At this point, it was not lack of attention or support that bothered the Newton team, it was the loss of uninterrupted time to work toward completion in a concentrated fashion. The deadline demands for getting the job done were bad enough without the added hours and effort that had to be devoted to bringing others from PIE up to speed. **Personal lives were shelved and the task at hand became the only thing on which the Newton team could concentrate.** Psychologist Karimi understood the sacrifice that was required and "con-

IN the Paris Metro, an indigent Parisian attempts conversation with Michael Tchao, who unfortunately understands little French. October 1992.

the Mac, Newton "required huge sacrifices on the part of so many people involved with it." He appreciated what it took for "an assemblage of some wonderful, talented people to agree to set aside their personal lives for several years to work together on a team, to go and do breakthrough work like this. It literally requires you to reach inside of yourself emotionally and find some inner talent, inner strength to get you through this."

The pressure was tough enough for singles who were unable to get out and socialize beyond the confines of Apple, but it was even harder on married couples. In fact, from the project's start, there was barely time to get married, even if plans were already set—as was the case for Capps and Marie D'Amico, an Apple attorney whom he had met when he gave her a deposition for an Apple copyright infringement lawsuit against Microsoft. One sunny September Sunday in 1991, Capps took a road-trip to Monterey to marry D'Amico. **Tchao was the only witness to a snap ceremony held in Monterey County, where no blood tests were required. Capps, still in his black wedding shorts, got back to the office in time to hack code for the rest of the night.**

sciously set aside all the other activities that required a little reflection—reading papers, going to conferences, interacting with colleagues at the professional level. I have left very little free time for myself. I don't know how long I'll be able to last."

Sculley, too, understood the toll of stress and the price paid by those working to bring Newton to market. He had seen a similar, single-minded commitment once before at Apple, during the development of Macintosh. Like

The twenty-seven-year-old, tambourine-playing Isono also took off a few days before CES in May 1992 to marry a young woman from Japan. New to the United States and having limited English facility, she spent many of her newlywed days at Apple, sitting patiently by her husband as he concentrated on his computer screen, something he did with devoted fervor.

Karen Sipprell, the PIE Division's marketing communications director, admitted she made a few concessions to her job "working eighteen hours a day." Getting ready to leave the office after yet another late evening, she reflected that her husband was not "happy when I come home like a wet dishrag, and I'm not even getting all my work done, so it's sort of not working out on either front. I haven't quite figured out how to balance that yet. But we're trying."

Capps eventually opted to integrate his personal and professional lives completely. A year after his wedding, he decided to work at his hilltop home, a twenty-minute drive from the office in his Honda featuring a palindromic "NOOTOON" license plate. He found that he was able to accomplish much more at his private desk than he could when people dropped by the office to ask questions. By October 1992 he had wired his house for Ethernet, a remote electronic link to the office network computer, and he was able to crank out code while directly connected to the rest of the office and the other engineers. The remote collaboration broadened when he invited Gannholm, a programmer, to come and help him—and then allowed him to take up indefinite residence in a spare room.

Romance was in the air *chez* Capps. Walter Smith, a graduate student who quit his Ph.D. program at Carnegie-Mellon University to join the Newton team, was spending a lot of time up at Capps' house helping the two resident hackers. He became so well-acquainted with D'Amico's female friend living in Capps' garden cottage that he ended up spending nearly all his time there. With so many people living so closely at the casual compound, it was inevitable that there would be a number of morning naked "butt sightings," which everyone reported and D'Amico tallied with amusement. Behinds aside, Smith's move to the cottage allowed him, Capps and Gannholm to work more efficiently, taking only an occasional break to drive south to Cupertino for a basketball game. When the hour was too late for shooting hoops outside, the three would often walk down to the garage for a 2:00 a.m. ping-pong match before getting down to real work—the all-night hack sessions required to make deadline.

Everyone felt the pressure mounting. By November, it was disappoint-ingly clear that Newton would not be ready by any stretch of the imagination for Christmas sales. The 1992 deadline for Newton's completion came and went. It was not clear at that point whether Newton would ever be ready at all. Some technical problems had proved recalcitrant. Difficulties with hand-writing recognition, user interface work and data storage all turned out to be far more complex than anybody ever had anticipated. **But the Newton team, numb to any pain at this point, rose to the challenges, accepted the added stress and worked even harder.** The reality of the situation in personal practical terms, was, as Sipprell said, that "You'd be very hard pressed to be in a division like this and have any priority other than what you're doing at work. Which is why I'm constantly in conflict. Because it's really not what my whole life is about."

Michael Tibbott, Newton's manager of quality and software tools, had worked on a number of projects for start-up companies in the past and felt that at Apple, "Somehow the pressure is more than it's been at other places. I think, to be honest, it's the people around here. We don't want to let them down. It's the Steve Cappses of the world who are working their twenty-hour days, which I couldn't physically do, but I feel guilty if I'm not working my sixteen-hour days or whatever. So you just don't want to let those people down. So I don't think it's driven by money or power. It's driven by people who think, 'You know, this is really cool.'"

Certainly, no material reward could be considered motivation enough for people to give up sleep, food, their most important relationships and their health. There was, as Tibbott hinted, something else that drove Capps and the whole Newton team to sacrifice nearly everything to meet deadlines dictated by marketing's assessment of the sales window of opportunity. They had bought into the vision. It was the knowledge that they were working on a product that was, as Sculley would repeat over and over, "revolutionary." It would actually get out the door to consumers and would not be stuck in the labs, where only a select few could appreciate its beauty.

Many programmers and engineers can take an enormous amount of abuse and develop a capacity to tolerate suffering for the cause of their work. Others cannot. The emotional and physical stress of hacking code late into the night can add to any existing instability. A horrifying tragedy for the tightly knit engineering group came at the end of 1992.

SANTA has a drink at a subdued Newton Christmas party. After the euphoria of a successful product concept introduction the previous May, Newton team members were daunted at year-end by the gargantuan and increasingly tedious task of building Newton. December 1992.

IT'S 1:00 a.m. and Ko Isono is pulling another all-nighter to solve a problem with the "inker." At 27, Isono was one of the youngest programmers on the team, and he felt the pressures of his complex life and the Newton project intensely. On December 12, 1992, he took his own life.

0 0 : 7 9

On December 12th, Capps received a cryptic message on his voice mail at work from Isono's wife, who had never before telephoned him. He saved the message, it was so strange. A few minutes later, the phone rang. It was one of Isono's friends asking if the news was true. At that moment, Donna Auguste, Newton's software manager, looking stricken, walked into Capps' Cupertino office, and he told the caller, "Yes, I think this is true," knowing by the look on Auguste's face that the devoted and sincere Isono was dead.

Capps found out that Isono, who habitually "worked crazy hours and stayed up late," left the Apple offices late after having been "up all night, went home, and he went into the bedroom and shot himself." The Japanese native commented to a colleague just a few weeks earlier: "You know what is great about the United States? You can buy guns."

Isono's suicide could easily have been the death of Newton. His stunned friends, reeling from their shock and sorrow, asked themselves over and over again what could have led him to such overwhelming despair. On the day of the funeral, it rained harder than it had in nearly a decade. If there was ever a time to sing the blues, it had just arrived.

Newton. Onstage. Live. The lights dim as expectations rise. Thousands crowd a cavernous Las Vegas hall to see what Newton can do live. Regardless of the numerous rehearsals that may precede, live performance always carries with it the risk of failure at a crucial moment.

A hush falls over the audience—an anticipatory silent moment—until the crowd breaks into applause as Newton takes the stage. Here is a performer with a polished look and timeless sound. Flawless. Wayne Newton's name will always be synonymous with Las Vegas.

On the other side of town from the prominently lighted Wayne Newton marquee, Apple's Alpha version of the Newton was rehearsing at the nearly empty convention center. The Alpha was an initial version of the machine in which all features were completed. While the performer who made his fame singing about red roses and blue ladies is allowed the occasional off-night, Apple's Newton had only one shot at the Vegas stage, and that live performance had to be great; it could not falter and still expect to be asked back for an extended engagement.

Industry critics were looking either to hail the new technology or con-demn Apple for promising more than it could deliver. Newton already had been announced and demonstrated at CES the previous spring, but momentum had slowed. Questions to Apple brought few direct answers from its public relations and marketing departments. In fact, Apple's coy, oblique responses raised new industry questions and fueled criticism in the trade press. *Digital Media* would sum it up best by headlining a piece, "Newton: A Study in Vagueness."

When the Newton core team members, now headed by PIE Division general manager Gaston Bastiaens, showed up for their first gig in Vegas, they were facing fierce competition, intense industry scrutiny and the nervous energy created by the knowledge that their equipment might not work.

. . . . .

"I think the nice thing in this environment is that all the seats are bare. People all are very creative. People all want to make the next great thing on earth. The art is to let them play as a team, instead of being all great individuals. That's the danger of a culture where individual prestige and contribution to creativity is so important that you only focus on the importance of the individual and not on the importance of the team and the business." — GASTON BASTIAENS

CORPORATE Director of Sharp, Apple's manufacturing partner, Akira Mitarai, lost in thought prior to giving a speech as part of a Newton demo and press briefing at the Las Vegas Consumer Electronics Show. January 1993.

NEW to Apple, Gaston Bastiaens faces the twin tasks of leading the recently formed PIE Division and making sure its most eagerly anticipated product, Newton, ships on time. He is moving rapidly to form partnerships and licensing agreements for Newton along with developing other PIE projects.

A month before the January Vegas convention, California was getting soaked. Relentless rains would bring the state out of its drought but would never force Steve Capps out of his signature shorts and sneakers. After seven years of drought, the climatic change was as welcome as Capps' sartorial consistency was remarkable.

Change and bold initiative seemed to be the primary themes that winter. Bill Clinton, with the highly visible support of Sculley, defeated George Bush in an election that pitted a computer-literate governor against a president surprised by supermarket checkout scanners. E-mail and fax technology allowed Clinton's team to respond rapidly to attack and take the information initiative. The Arkansas governor's campaign staff was well-equipped with cellular phones and knew how to use on-line services to stay one step ahead of Bush.

The country was talking about a technology policy and data highways. Sculley was rumored to be up for a Clinton cabinet post. Things suddenly began to look a bit more hopeful, so much so that even the laggard economy appeared to improve slightly.

Any positive mood shift was important for the Newton team following the traumatic news of Isono's death. The team had already been pushed to the limits and Tibbott felt that it "was a pretty bad time. It was amazing that we didn't just explode." Instead, the team buckled down even more. Tibbott believed that "maybe that was the best therapy, just to keep working hard."

Still, Tibbott and other technical team managers "were very worried about lots of people. We actually went around to the software managers and talked about every person in the group in terms of 'Is this person on the edge? Should we do a buddying-up with these people to see if they are okay?' It was a very, very interesting kind of psychological triage."

The subdued mood at the PIE division's Christmas party at the end of 1992 was a good indicator that people were still shocked by their colleague's death. Depression was not far away, either, when they looked back on a year in which they had been unable to deliver on their technical promises.

With a month left before the January Vegas convention, Tricia Chan, a public relations specialist for Newton, surveyed the crowd at the Christmas party from her corner of the room. Her job was to control not only the information fed to the press, but to understand and occasionally manage the dynamics of the disparate groups working on Newton.

Chan's attention jumped to a man who bounced all about the room, moving from clique to clique, huddling with two people at a time. This perpetually moving person was a mystery man for most of the Newton group. This was the first time many had laid eyes on Bastiaens, a Belgian who left his job as director of the Consumer Electronics Division and general manager of the Interactive Media Systems Group at Philips Electronics in Eindhoven, Netherlands, to come and head the PIE division. Newton was now his baby. He would cap or break his career with the success or failure of this new technology, his big opportunity to prove to himself and the world that his achievements could be as great as his ambition. The Newton team saw in Bastiaens a man who was exacting and compulsively driven, the ideal combination of traits to keep creative tension high.

Bastiaens arrived at Apple just a few weeks before Isono's death and was preparing to push Newton's development and public demonstrations

even harder. **He told some software engineers that he expected a miracle.** During the Christmas party, he reminded the Newton team that they would go for broke with a Newton Alpha version during CES three weeks later. Even the Manhattan Project seemed to be on a leisurely schedule compared to the round-the-clock demands Bastiaens placed on Newton's designers and support staff. The overworked and emotionally exhausted team cut loose for a dance or two, but many realized that the cramming had only just begun and decided to leave the party early.

Bastiaens was a wryly smiling, deal-cutting executive whose last product launch had centered around Philips' interactive compact disc technology. He arrived at Apple with a mandate to lead his division into the company's future, one that would rely not on hardware sales, but on annuity income generated from software, online and publishing services. He told people he

KAREN Sipprell, PIE Marketing and Communications Manager, helps stuff press kits which will be released during the Newton demo and progress report at the Las Vegas CES. With jobs at Microsoft and Steve Jobs' NeXT Computer under her belt, Sipprell is intimately familiar with the pressures associated with getting a high-tech product off the ground. January 1993.

0 0 : 7 3

was not out to win any popularity contests, but his laser-like focus on stated goals won him respect from even those who felt that his grasp of technical minutiae was minimal. Bastiaens was certainly not the only senior executive at Apple whose technical understanding was subject to criticism. Sculley, too, despite his competence, was still occasionally fighting a lingering industry perception that he was not enough of an engineer to run a high-tech company.

Bastiaens was a taskmaster, but he demanded no less of others than he did of himself. Starting a typical day before sunrise in his hillside home, he ran at a near-sprint for a few miles before settling down to the marathon of the day's deal-making. He followed his early morning routine by cruising down to Cupertino in his American dream machine—a Cadillac—while blasting country-and-western tunes on the stereo. The rest of the day was organized by one of his two administrative assistants, the first one working the morning-to-midday shift and the second taking over until late at night, when Bastiaens dropped by to visit the engineers before going home for a restful three to four hours' sleep.

Even though Newton was progressing at a steady pace, Chan knew that in the public eye, Newton's momentum and enthusiasm were slowing.

Bastiaens realized that Apple's reputation of the past decade would be put to a serious test in a matter of weeks. In business, he was a high-stakes gambler. How fitting that Vegas would be the venue for him to make the technological crapshoot.

Chan's job was to lower public expectations while still promising a breakthrough and adding to the overall Newton message. Positioning Newton as a great personal communications device—eventually filling the roles of the mobile phone, fax and pager—required a move away from handwriting recognition, which was temperamental technology. Her job was no cakewalk, but then again, neither was the job of designing this increased functionality. She would occasionally stop by Capps' house to visit her friend D'Amico, and she noticed that the engineer saw everything as a surmountable challenge. Capps remained perversely sunny. Chan admired his brilliance and his ability to act confident in the face of constant system crashes, battery drainings, cursive-writing non-recognition, infrared interference and last-minute icon changes. These difficulties sometimes caused Chan to operate in a state of controlled panic. How were they possibly going to get ready for Vegas?

· · · · ·

TRICIA Chan, public relations whiz, checks on a colleague's arrival while event producer Michael Witlin hits the floor in a show of exasperation prior to a CES Newton demo and press briefing. January 1993.

Newton team members trickled into Vegas as early as they could, with Capps flying in the night before the Newton demonstration. Below him, the distant lights blinked in the night, an incandescent oasis beckoning those with plenty to bet and even more to lose.

A quick check of the clock in the Las Vegas International Airport terminal indicated that show-time was only hours away. Capps stayed up all night making sure phone and fax lines were working, checking and re-checking connections, hacking last-minute software changes.

In the morning, Chan asked him to join the group and meet a psychologist who had come to conduct a mock news conference, an aggressive question-and-answer session with a critical press demanding to know when Newton would be available. Although Capps was physically in the room, he had checked out mentally and was sprawled out in his chair, eyes shut, mouth agape. He was as tired as he was wired.

Testing the five Alpha prototype versions of Newton was continuous, rehearsing and re-rehearsing the features and communications functions that were going to be highlighted. Capps and Tchao were working with the machines with some success—and the occasional crash. Rehearsal crashes were common, but it was always unnerving when too many skeptical journalists were milling about just outside the rehearsal hall. Chan was busy writing the day's press release and stuffing press packets until the last minute. The pressure was palpable. Someone came up to Capps and told him he had to check an urgent E-mail message. He wanted to disconnect one of Capps' onstage fax lines to hook up his computer. Capps momentarily lost his cool.

Bastiaens arrived with Apple's new strategic partners, the Japanese representatives from Sharp. He knew that the demonstration about to take place had to impress Sharp as much as it did the industry news media.

"Part of what doing business in the '90s is about for everybody is having alliances and also having competition. I mean, you can see it in our relationship with IBM—we're partners in two deals and we're competing with each other in the marketplace. Obviously with Sharp, we have a very close relationship. They're dependent on us for software; we're dependent on them for the actual hardware manufacturing, and we will be competing in the marketplace." — BARRY SCHIFFMAN

THE stress of preparing for the media is wearing on Burt Cummings as he reads the day's press release. January 1993.

0 0 : 6 9

SUSAN Schuman and Nazila Alasti listen as a psychologist/speech coach conducts a mock media question-and-answer session while Steve Capps catches up on some much needed sleep before the Newton demonstration. January 1993.

REPORTERS mob the stage seeking a closer look at Newton after the demonstration. January 1993.

0 0 : 6 8

Bastiaens tended to be flamboyant amidst the Fourth Estaters and promised results and technical developments that seemed humanly unattainable by the often-extemporaneous deadlines he declared. There was another drawback to setting him loose on the American press: his accent. It was thick and hard to understand. And the language he spoke was not always exactly English.

Bastiaens gave a speech about communications that some American journalists did not fully comprehend. Tchao and Capps were then called to the stage for the demonstration. Unlike the show at the summer CES, this one would be done only from a handheld unit not attached to a Macintosh. The Newton unit was battery-powered, entirely self-contained and subject to random failure.

There was no time to worry whether the technology would work. There was only the moment and the silence of the audience. Newton team members were a collective coiled nerve. Capps whipped out his stylus and started cursive writing on Newton. Bang. It was translated into typeface. Success. Nods from the first row. Chan knew the first hurdle had been cleared.

Capps then started drawing shapes, the symmetry of which Newton recognized and then cleaned up. He drew a house with a—oops, "that was

MICHAEL Tchao and Steve Capps show fists full of Newtons to the media after demonstrating Newton technology. January 1993.

supposed to be a door"—and a window, a chimneystack. He then tried to fax the—oops, well, "let's use the router"—to fax the note with the picture of the house. Demonstrating the fax capability was hit or miss on any day, particularly with technology that had only recently made it to the initial, Alpha level. Capps waited for his fax to go through.

A pregnant pause. Nothing was happening. The fax machine rang; Capps maintained his outward cool. Chan's guts were wrenching. Nothing. The fax machine's light was blinking, but nothing was being spit out—until, finally, the strained machine sound of the fax cleared its throat and delivered the first blackened line on white thermal paper. Yes, the fax was working! Applause from the gallery. The audience had turned from skeptics to converts; Chan could feel it. All that was left now was a minor infrared cross-talk between two Newtons exchanging rudimentary information using the type of technology found in home-entertainment remote controls. This was basic, tried-and-true technology very familiar to everyone attending CES.

The demonstration failed.

The front row of engineers and journalists heaved a collective sigh. Chan needed to prepare for a rapid response. Newton was supposed to

"squirt" over the information that would emulate the exchange of business cards between two users. If successful, the "squirting" would have made a big splash with the journalists, but now it only served to increase doubts about a technology that minutes before had seemed flawless.

After the demonstration, despite the failures, journalists crowded around the platform, excited, shooting questions rapid-fire. Capps and company handled the queries perfectly. Their belief and commitment to the technology shone through. Chan, in the meantime, was working on damage control to make sure not too much was made of the "squirting" fiasco.

She pulled Capps aside and asked him if he could try the infrared demonstration again. His eyes lit up. Sure, he said, he could do it. Tchao heard this and told Capps, "No way, no way!"—begging him not to try. Tchao had to know that while one failure is bad, reinforcing that failure could be disastrous. No, Capps argued, he thought he knew what went wrong.

Chan pulled together a group of journalists from daily newspapers and set up an impromptu demonstration while Capps was still fiddling with the Newtons.

Capps continued to work with the two machines and tapped a couple of commands that appeared on the screen. With no sound or motion emanating from Newton, it was hard to tell if anything was happening. Infrared is invisible to the human eye and barely fathomable to the brain. There was, however, a more immediate way to tell if the technology was working—by the expression on Capps' face and the reactions from Tchao and Chan. Stillness and silence were broken as a smile rose on Capps' face. After everyone had left the room, Tchao and Chan leaped up, slapping each other high-fives.

The press was charmed and Chan spun the journalists until they were dizzily giddy about Newton. On a day when the Dow Jones industrial average took a steep, twenty-point dive, exuberant press reports helped push Apple's stock up by one and one-half points. **Bastiaens' gamble had paid off. Newton would not be relegated to the borscht belt.**

A bellman waits for Michael Tchao to make a note on his Newton on his way to check in to his hotel in Hannover, Germany. His Newton is running Alpha software. March 1993.

0 0 : 6 1

Showstopping performance is important in event marketing. But, as the Newton group found out, each successful performance raises the bar for subsequent stunts. In the months leading up to Newton's scheduled July 29th launch date, its public demonstrations increased in both frequency and level of difficulty. Sipprell understood the stakes and pressures of the endgame and characterized the PIE division mood as "insane right now. It's really, really out of control."

Adding to the stress on the Newton crew was its displacement at the beginning of 1993, when its offices were moved from the familiar warehouse on Bubb Road to a shiny, new, glass-and-steel building a couple of miles away, part of an Apple research and development complex on a street called "Infinite Loop"—an inside joke that Newton's engineers did not find funny, since "infinite loop" refers to a bug in which a program endlessly executes a routine, preventing anything else from getting completed. Along with the new surroundings came new people, the added members of a growing PIE division of which Newton was now only one part—albeit the central one.

Bastiaens' arrival as PIE's leader and his increasingly aggressive posture at the beginning of 1993 coincided with the diminution of Tesler's influence

over the engineers. On April 9th, it was announced that Tesler would return to Apple's Advanced Technology Group as the company's Chief Scientist, the division he had led before coming to Newton. On his last day in the office, with boxes full of books and files stacked outside his door, he had no confidence that a good-enough product would go out the door, because "there is still a lot to do to get it to be perfect enough to put into a run and ship it to customers." Tesler felt the product would have to be as close to perfect as possible before hitting the store shelves, and he was skeptical that the software would go through enough testing and correcting before Bastiaens' manufacturing deadlines.

As 1993 got underway, Apple produced every imaginable variation on the Macintosh theme, including a series of laptop PowerBooks and new desktop Color Classics. But more products did not mean more income. Industry-wide competition shoved down Apple's profits to about half its late-1980s margins of over 50 percent. Apple needed an income infusion soon, and the company was counting on the delayed Newton and the rest of the PIE Division's products to start earning their keep.

Bastiaens pushed the Newton team harder than ever to meet its new deadlines and achieve his single-minded goal of success. The next major public demonstration took place in mid-March at Europe's largest computer forum, CeBIT (the German acronym for the World Expo Center for Office, Information and Telecommunication Systems), in Hannover, Germany.

When Tchao and Nazila Alasti, a Newton product line manager, walked past a Bavarian beer garden and into the presentation hall, they were greeted with a daily CeBIT newsletter that pictured a PDA on its cover with the headline "First to Market?" The article was about a PDA manufactured by Amstrad, an English computer company, priced at £299.99, including VAT—about $350 below the $799 expected price for Apple's MessagePad.

PDA, of course, was the acronym Sculley had coined in his January 1992 CES speech, when he had introduced a new product for a market that did not yet exist. In the intervening fifteen months, the term PDA had become almost generic, used loosely by any company wishing to differentiate its products from the organizer market that Sharp and Casio dominated with their Wizard and B.O.S.S. pocket machines. Although the Amstrad product announcement came as a shock to Tchao—after all, Newton at that point was still four-and-a-half months away from being launched—he also took it as proof that Newton's

MICHAEL Tchao arrives in Hannover with ten working Newtons running Alpha software. Tchao will participate in a press briefing at CeBIT. March 1993.

"We're at the juncture right now where we know how we're positioning this. We're calling it a mobile communicator with intelligent assistance. And that's slightly different from what we said originally—that it's a personal digital assistant. You know, John went out and coined this term, PDA, but since that time, we've seen all of the organizers in the world glom on to PDA. They started running ads—the Sharp Wizard, the Casio B.O.S.S. and everything else. And, actually, what we found when we did research was that intelligent assistance was the most important product attribute to people. It came out higher than price, which practically never happens, according to the research company. What we have to do is differentiate—and that will keep us out of the organizer category." — KAREN SIPPRELL

MICHAEL Tchao and his marketing colleagues Nazila Alasti and Susan Schuman test Newtons prior to a CeBIT press briefing. Tchao brought ten working Alpha units. Seven are still working. March 1993.

GASTON Bastiaens delivers last-minute words of advice to Michael Tchao and Nazila Alasti, backs to camera, before the press briefing and Newton demonstration for the European press. March 1993.

MICHAEL Tchao and Nazila Alasti stride toward the stage to take part in the CeBIT Newton demonstration and progress report. March 1993.

NEWTON event producer Michael Witlin whispers a
stage command to his crew during the CeBIT press
briefing by Apple executives Gaston Bastiaens and
Michael Spindler, seen in background on stage.

0 0 : 5 3

potential market was being taken seriously. "If imitation is the highest form of flattery," he declared grumpily, "then we are very flattered."

Tchao wondered aloud if there was a way to sue for "flagrant flattery or flattery with intent." The issue of copyright infringement was a sore one for Apple. Since March 1988, it had been embroiled in a protracted lawsuit against Microsoft, which it accused of infringing on the proprietary "look and feel" of the Macintosh operating system. Microsoft's highly successful Windows software program for DOS machines allowed IBM personal computers and their clones to operate in a manner that approximated Macintosh's easy-to-use graphical user interface, Apple argued. Later in the year, Apple finally lost the suit.

Tchao's half-joking thought of suing a company for copying a product that Apple had not even released pointed to the belief of many Apple marketing specialists that the Newton market's window of opportunity was closing quickly. Sculley's announcement of Apple's intentions—rather than the actual product—more than a year before the arrival of the Newton technology had allowed competitors to enter early in the race to the PDA market.

The Talking Heads' driving rhythm and the lyrics "Stop making sense"

PRESS and fairgoers gather and wait to see the Newton progress report and demonstration. March 1993.

were piped into the dim CeBIT exhibition room where the Newton team was about to present a progress report to a few hundred invited journalists. Apple usually drew strong crowds, but this day's solid turnout was helped by the announcement that a home-team player had joined with the kids from California. Siemens, a German telecommunications, electronics and computer firm, recently had become a major partner in the Newton effort. **The venerable company hoped to profit from its association with a new product having as much revolutionary potential as the Macintosh.** And Apple hoped Siemens would provide the credibility and stability that the California company might have lacked otherwise in the conservative German business environment.

Before members of the press were ushered into the presentation, they gossiped outside while downing complimentary glasses of wine. A couple of German journalists, both stout, belligerent men, proffered loud, disparaging remarks about Apple before entering the hall.

Once the hall was full, the presentation began. Siemens' bigwigs sat in the front row and listened to their countryman, Apple's president Michael Spindler—a former Siemens employee himself—speak about the importance of the German company's support and collaboration. According to Susan Schuman, Apple's manager of product planning and strategy and communication products, Siemens had felt a little uneasy about its relations with Apple ever since General Magic had announced a partnership with Apple and AT&T—Siemens' largest competitor. Apple had all but sealed its partnership arrangement with Siemens before the General Magic announcement, said Schuman, and then had failed to let Siemens know that the new, larger General Magic consortium of companies included the U.S. communications giant. The breakneck pace of partner and licensee deal-cutting had caused diplomacy to fall by the wayside.

Much of Newton's partnering and licensing had taken place in a whirlwind eight- to twelve-week period, driven by Bastiaens. According to Subra Iyer, PIE's licensing business manager, there was no time to finesse deals or be as diplomatic as he would have liked with those already aboard. Bastiaens' strategy, implemented by Iyer and Apple attorney David Farrington, was to get as many people to sign on to Newton technology as quickly as possible in an effort to provide the product with the momentum and support it would need if it were to establish itself as the standard. Apple had already succeeded

"Culturally, I would say the biggest difference that impacts the way we do business—and there are many—is that the Japanese tend to be more organized and more structured in their thought process. For example, many Japanese firms write a specification before they even start product development. Many American firms ship the product and then write the specification. So, there's a very fundamental mindset difference going on, especially in the Newton group."

— Vikki Pachera

in getting a number of partners aboard for various purposes: Motorola was developing a pager card for Newton products, and a down-to-the-wire five-week negotiation brought BellSouth onto the team to provide messaging services. Random House was an early supporter, looking for Newton electronic publishing opportunities.

Apple told its partners that it was looking for as broad a licensing arrangement as possible, in which many companies would be included, but Iyer later understood that a number of early partners wanted to believe they would be consulted or informed about any Apple decisions to expand its licensing and partnering. Schuman said that Apple's deal with AT&T and General Magic "went to the last minute and was signed just short of midnight" with no consideration paid to its other partners. The carelessness caused by the pace of this type of activity and Apple's inexperience was showing. With limited partnering experience and staff to make the deals, Apple was just trying to keep its head above what appeared to be murky business waters.

Siemens was not the only foreign company that year to receive unwelcome news about the California company's alliances. Sharp, another of Apple's strategic partners, received a surprise on the day of the Newton CeBIT presentation, when Shintaro Hashimoto, one of the Japanese company's vice presidents, saw representatives of Matsushita in the presentation room. They were hard to miss, since they were sitting right across from him. **Matsushita, which manufactures Panasonic products, is one of Sharp's fiercest rivals and was about to be introduced as a new licensee of Newton technology.** There was considerable discomfort on the part of the Sharp team when Bastiaens announced the new partnership. Onstage, however, Hashimoto remained composed, and diplomatically stated that Sharp and Apple were "competitors in the marketplace and partners in the research labs." The representatives of both Japanese companies, seated opposite each other on either side of the center aisle, seldom looked across but studiously videotaped the other's presentations and speeches onstage.

And then, finally, it was Newton's moment in the limelight. Tchao had to know that if the demonstration failed, his baby would be taken to task as a bogus product made by a company that held little sentimental appeal for this mostly German audience—a critical, knowledgeable crowd that was neither prone to swooning over Apple's technology nor enchanted by the company founded in a California garage.

Schuman took the stage to demonstrate the machine. Things rapidly fell apart. Her MessagePad refused to behave. She attempted to show its phoning capabilities while using the attached Siemens modem, but when she wrote "Ring Dietrich," the screen interpreted her stylus pressure as an unintelligible scribble. Schuman, pink with embarrassment but prepared for such an eventuality, pulled out a spare MessagePad from under the dais, but the new machine had the same problems. Finally, after a few tries, it cooperated, phoning "Dietrich," a German stage presence, and faxing a prepared message.

It was a Pyrrhic success, though, and a gnat-like audience member kept whining, "I have a question, I have a question." Schuman ignored him in the same way politicians pretend not to hear embarrassing queries. Her antagonist persisted until Schuman turned to tell him coolly, "I think we're taking questions at the end." The response elicited cynical laughter. Siemens' austere executives shifted uneasily in their seats.

Tchao and Alasti quickly took things over from Schuman. In addition to demonstrating the gadget, the ethnically diverse pair also conveyed to the audience a subtle cultural message about how Newton's hiring practices differed from the German norm—and how Newton would serve an international buyership. Newton's software manager, Donna Auguste—a high-tech rarity as a female engineer, or "*black* female engineer," as she emphasizes—had achieved success despite the industry's male domination. She observed that vastly varied points of view and people were essential for the product's development. She knew that Newton, to succeed, would have to be created "for people who don't care what the technology is, they just want it to be useful to them. This means we have to look at it from a lot more perspectives than just the 'white male nerd' perspective or we're going to fail. The problem-solving of allowing it to be adaptive for people of different cultures calls for the willingness and ability to look at it from different perspectives."

At the end of the Tchao-Alasti presentation, Bastiaens took the stage. Questions from the audience started with a combative tone.

"How much will it cost?"

"Well below $1,000."

"Will it be below £299?"—a stinging reference to the Amstrad PDA

APPLE Personal Interactive Electronics Division chief Gaston Bastiaens holds his own with an aggressive European press after a live demonstration and Newton progress report at the CeBIT Computer Faire. March 1993.

0 0 : 4 7

announced earlier in the day, which was being showcased on the CeBIT convention showroom floor.

"Significantly below $1,000."

"Will it ever be available? Or is Apple just going to keep announcing that it will be available?"

Bastiaens told the questioner to give him his name and address because he was ready to wager him. "I bet my wine cellar on this: The Newton will be available this summer." This was a significant move, given that Bastiaens has a large and eclectic collection of wines.

One of the two bellicose German journalists, who earlier had made nasty cracks about Apple outside, piped up. "This is only a toy. Until you have voice recognition, it will remain a toy!"

At that point, Spindler took the microphone. "Give us a break." **With the measured, confident tone of a schoolteacher, the Apple president reminded the audience that voice recognition was tough to perfect and that it was "barely available on $30,000 machines."** Bastiaens, taking over the microphone from Spindler, then tried to spin the problem into

a win by adding that Newton was designed to allow the addition of any reliably developed voice recognition system that might be available in the future.

Leaving Bastiaens onstage, Spindler stepped off, and clearly perturbed by the voice-recognition dig, blurted to surprised Apple bystanders, "Who was that fat asshole?"

If Spindler's reaction was defensive, Bastiaens' response showed that he

liked to go head-on with skeptics. "Look, I'm being honest with you," he cajoled the audience. "This is the Alpha version. If we had Beta here, you would be impressed." Then, abruptly, he announced, "Today, we are freezing Beta."

Engineers use the first two letters of the Greek alphabet as benchmarks for the stages of software development. "Alpha" is a version in which all the included features are completed. "Beta" means that the system should no longer crash. The final stage is when software achieves "Golden Master" status, meaning that it has no bugs and is ready to be sold to the public.

Although the Beta version of the Newton operating system technically was frozen once Bastiaens said so, bugs kept showing up in the code and sometimes caused the system to crash. Also, engineers failed to respect the sanctity of Bastiaens' freeze and kept adding features. The irrepressible Capps was busy tinkering with already functioning code, doing the equivalent of tight editing on coherent but voluminous lines of text. He was trying to turn Thomas Mann into Ernest Hemingway. And he was doing this primarily for aesthetic reasons: He did not like the way the code looked. "It's like saying, 'Hey, look at my neat, new car, but don't worry about the interior—it's all messed up,'" he explained. "We're taking code that works perfectly fine, and we're changing it." There was just one problem. What he was doing, though reversible, had the potential to ruin Newton's existing code. If the code worked after his changes and no new bugs appeared, no one would be upset. But plenty of people were nervous about the potential for disaster that such changes created.

As a result of Capps' work, screen-surfing always seemed to hold unwelcome surprises for Tibbott, who was in charge of making sure software for the MessagePad met its deadlines. **He had to get Capps to stop, and he urged Capps' wife "to just bodily drag Capps away for a while, 'cause I think for him to relax is to go and write some other part of the software that he's not responsible for."** Shortly after CeBIT, Tibbott discovered an unexpected Newton feature, a thermometer that gauged the MessagePad's internal temperature. Tibbott surmised that it had been added late one night for no other reason than "because Capps had half an hour to play. So, we're totally surprised to find this, and that's actually a big problem. We really need to stop doing stuff like that. You don't want to stifle him, but at some point, you just say, 'Enough is enough!' It's like, 'Walk away, go for a walk, get out of there!'"

The Newton software team realized it had to stop noodling around with new features and get down to work presenting a final candidate for Golden Master if Newton was ever going to make its May 26th manufacturing deadline with a ROM that was bug- and crash-free. Capps and company, often ignoring Tibbott's ban on creative additions, worked as close to around-the-clock as they could. As usual, they were on a burnout schedule. The only way to mark time at the Infinite Loop One building was by watching the movement of the sun, counting the days down to official launch, or by measuring the progress of finding and zapping computer bugs.

On the securely locked second floor, near the mailboxes and junk food-filled kitchen, a Macintosh Classic II sat silently flashing a reminder of how many bugs had been identified. "As of 5/5, Total Bugs to Date: 3,278." Many had been zapped, but according to the on-screen graph, there were still well over a thousand bugs left to kill. There was an added incentive for bug-catchers: the discovery of each error in another person's code would earn a gift certificate from Apple management for CDs at Tower Records.

Deadline dates slipped by and Newton gained a "vaporware" reputation among technology pundits and the press. Novelty items started appearing at industry shows, mocking Apple's product. "Nuttin" was a simple notepad with a pencil attached to its side. A badge with a yellow drawing of a Fig Newton surrounded by the international symbol for "not," the circle with a diagonal slash, was seen on the jackets and backpacks of Newton naysayers.

By the end of May, it was clear that the Golden Master software that was supposed to be burned into ROM would not be finished on time. Vikki Pachera, the program manager for Newton products, knew that any deadlines Apple missed would throw off Sharp's schedule, too. She had worked with the Japanese at Apple for more than six years. "The Japanese tend to meet their commitments. When they say it's going to be done on Tuesday, it's done on Tuesday. When we say it's going to be done on Tuesday, well, Tuesday or Friday."

In light of the deadline problems, Bastiaens made a compromise decision to manufacture 4,000 ROMs including only Beta-level software, instead of renegotiating the entire manufacturing schedule to wait for Golden Master-level software. The 4,000 units would not be sold to consumers, but would be used in retail shops' point-of-purchase displays.

JOHN Sculley, Gaston Bastiaens and members of the PIE division and Newton team watch a demonstration of Newton Beta software at a party for departing Newton team leader Larry Tesler. April 1993.

Consumer confidence ebbed a few months after Clinton took office, partly because of the uncertainty about the effect of proposed new taxes, but also because there was no noticeable change in the economy or the gridlock in which the Congress and administration were stuck. On a macroeconomic level, bilateral and trade relations with Japan also affected the consumer electronics market, and Clinton's team was talking a hardball trade-restriction game while slacking on the basics of getting a U.S. ambassador in place. The balance of trade still favored Japan, while currency rates fluctuated, threatening consumer product price increases if the yen/dollar relationship did not stabilize. Industry leaders were reserved, and the Tandy Corporation's chairman stated in an interview at the June CES that he expected "unexceptional performance" by everyone in the consumer electronics market for the rest of 1993.

Superstores that specialize in overwhelming customers with walls of television sets all tuned to the same station and hundreds of VCRs were having a hard time moving products that spring. But they were already planning their fall advertising supplements. The multi-page store ads that come tumbling out of Sunday morning newspapers are produced three months ahead of time, and Apple promised to provide both pictures and copy for the MessagePad, which was supposed to be available by August. Tchao knew that the worst possible scenario would be for these new distribution channels to advertise an Apple product that was not yet on their store shelves.

. . . . .

Storm clouds hovered outside the forty-sixth floor of Chicago's posh Four Seasons Hotel on June 3rd as speechwriter Arynne Simon and PIE public relations specialists Tricia Chan and Frank O'Mahony re-read speeches, stuffed PR packages and commiserated over the discouraging news that the Tandy-Casio Zoomer organizer had been announced that morning. A story was featured prominently on the front page of the day's *Chicago Tribune* business section, with only a passing reference to the delayed Newton product.

Downstairs, in the Grand Ballroom, Tchao and James Joaquin, the Newton product line manager of software and tools development, were trying to decide what they were going to demonstrate this time around. **The drill seemed stale to them by now, and they shot down ideas one after another.** Tchao was well into his rehearsal of a docking feature, transferring files from Newton to a Macintosh, when he caught a glimpse of the *Tribune's* Zoomer story: "Oh, my God!" He read each

word intently, obviously seeing a competitor's new product for the first time. Tchao pondered the consequences of the Zoomer announcement and the way consumers might confuse it with Newton. "We're now in an interesting position. We're first in rhetoric but second in product." Joaquin glanced at the newspaper article, then at Tchao. Dismissively, he concluded: "It looks like a Game Boy."

According to the article, the information permanently stored in the Zoomer included the U.S. Constitution, zodiac signs and birthstones. Tchao and Joaquin toyed with the idea of including their own birthstones in the Newton database demonstration—a direct, if somewhat petty, dig at the

NEWTON Program Manager Vikki Pachera joins other Newton team members at a farewell party for Larry Tesler. April 1993.

WORKBENCH in Newton engineering
lab. April 1993.

BUG hunt: Steve Capps and fellow software programmers Martin Gannholm, lower right, and Walter Smith are working around the clock at Capps' San Carlos, California, house, fixing bugs. They devour lots of Reese's peanut butter cups and sleep only during "builds"—the period of downtime needed for code compilation. Here, they are reading a message from their teammates at Apple alerting them to more bugs. April 1993.

machine that seemed destined to snatch part of Newton's market, not only by looking and behaving like the MessagePad, but also by being priced competitively. The scuttlebutt was that at whatever point the MessagePad was priced, the Zoomer would undercut it by $100.

Tchao was frustrated that Newton's software engineers were missing deadlines—and by the news that the product launch planned for the end of July had just been delayed until the first week of August. Immediately prior to CES, headquarters had flicked on the safety latch for the launch announcement, which, until then, they had insisted was "locked and loaded for July 29th." Newton would instead make its premiere a week later at the Boston Macworld, an annual, Apple-friendly gathering of Macintosh fans. But software builds were so late—and still occasionally crashing—that it was not clear to Tchao that Newton would meet its August 2nd deadline either.

Bastiaens was hoping Newton would sell out at Macworld and that its aura of success would encourage consumer desire—or, better yet, need. Bastiaens wanted the MessagePad to appear as a product people wanted so badly that supply could not keep up with demand. He also knew the best way to develop crucial positive word-of-mouth advertising was to get the product in the hands of the true believers, the segment of the market labeled "early adopters."

With less than an hour to go before the Newton progress report in Chicago, O'Mahony took the stage to rehearse his introduction and welcome: "They say that 85 percent of life is just throwing up. . ." Simon heard her words blown. She froze and looked up at the dais. ". . . That's 'showing up'", O'Mahony corrected himself, laughing. "Just kidding, I'll get it right."

Showing up just then at the ballroom door was a bearded, fortyish man carrying a plastic shopping bag and looking displaced as he wandered through the room, searching. Joaquin approached the stranger. "I'm sorry, this room is closed for rehearsal. Is there something I can help you with?"

NEWTON programmer Bob Welland suffers the indignity of having a parachuting school instructor choose his lap to sit on during a demonstration of proper tandem jumping techniques. Fellow programmers Daniel Culbert and Linda Yogi joined Welland in making their first jumps. The Newton team management was "not exactly thrilled" that they chose to learn a dangerous sport like skydiving while the product was still in development. April 1993.

"I am Stepan Pachikov with Paragraph. I am looking for Gaston."

Pachikov had developed the handwriting recognition software included in every Newton, and had negotiated a large unit royalty in the process. It seemed Apple would help turn former Soviet hackers into Russian millionaire entrepreneurs in no time. Pachikov's father was a military man and his family had lived in Soviet Georgia and Siberia before moving to Moscow, where Pachikov had founded Paragraph during the early days of Mikhail Gorbachev's glasnost. Paragraph was now a sizable company with offices in Colorado and a presence in Silicon Valley.

Pachikov had come to the hotel ballroom to find Bastiaens and clear up the terms of an agreement they had signed the day before. An unforeseen drama unfolded as Pachikov spotted Bastiaens and prevented him from getting onstage to rehearse his speech. They had to talk. Now. Pachikov was very unhappy. He said that he felt Apple's legal department had misled him after he and Bastiaens had agreed to certain contractual items. According to Pachikov's brother George, who had accompanied him, Stepan did not approve of a clause requiring Paragraph's cursive recognition to achieve 99.8 percent accuracy, particularly since past discussions always had targeted 95 percent as a medium-term goal. Stepan said he once told Bastiaens half-jokingly how difficult it would be to achieve absolutely perfect handwriting recognition: "Gaston, it is easier for me to develop a 110 percent accurate cursive handwriting recognizer than to explain to you why it can't be done."

Handwriting recognition was not improving quickly enough for the first product, Bastiaens liked to argue, and user studies showed that people were frustrated quickly by the machine's inability to pick out short words. Strangely enough, the shorter and simpler the word, the harder it was for the recognizer to understand it. **The longer the word, the more decipherable it was, since the recognizer had more information to use.** Complex, unusual, multisyllabic words like "xylophone" narrowed Newton's choices for possible words in its dictionary, unlike some of the more common, monosyllabic words in the English language, such as "I."

Fluid handwriting recognition was one of the main features that would differentiate Newton from other PDAs, including the Zoomer, but, of course, chronic faulty recognition could be worse than no recognition at all. Bastiaens, observing a user study the week before CES, decided that an instructional video would have to be provided with every Newton to explain

STEVE Capps is tired of meetings at Apple that keep him from his computer and writing code for Newton, so he is wiring his house with a high-speed data transfer link. April 1993.

how handwriting recognition should work and how the user could make it work better. This addition would cost around $1.50 more per unit sold and would pose new packaging problems for Newton. In addition, it would mean producing a snap, high-quality, twelve-minute, $100,000 movie that would have to reflect favorably on the product.

Bastiaens, looking as though he wished Pachikov would just leave him alone so he could get on with his rehearsal, picked up the phone to speak with the folks in Cupertino, trying to accommodate some of the Russian entrepreneur's more serious grievances. During earlier negotiations with Pachikov, Bastiaens always played the good cop to the legal department's bad cop. While an acceptable tactic, this was an apparent difference from the top-down directive school of management to which Pachikov had grown accustomed at home in the former Soviet Union. There, the higher up a decision was made, the less likely it was to be revised further down along the line of command. To Pachikov, the Apple legal department's ability to overrule Bastiaens was unthinkable. "Bastiaens is a vice president!"

Either Pachikov negotiated cleverly by acting innocent and victimized or he was genuinely startled to find that the amorphous legal department liked to make each Bastiaens concession a contractual point of contention. Apple's negotiator Iyer suspected the former was true: "Stepan is shrewd and he's a mathematician. He's great at playing this 'I don't understand the language' game at his convenience." In any case, Pachikov—who served as his company's own marketing head, PR director, programming chief and legal department—was pacing the ballroom when, ingeniously or not, he announced, "It's the last contract I sign with Apple."

The doors finally opened and the crowd slowly filed in, one of the journalists carrying the PDA made by GO, a number of others holding Zoomer press kits. **An inaccurate article published by *InfoWorld* reporting that the ready-to-sell Newton would be announced at this CES nearly doubled the planned attendance. Gone, however, was all the excitement of the year before, when Newton was first shown.** Instead, this skeptical crowd was drooping with ennui. Many had already seen a Newton demonstration, and most were only curious to see if there had been any significant new developments.

Tchao's demonstration went well. The infrared transfer of data had failed during rehearsal, prompting Tchao to tell Joaquin, "If we screw this up the way we did at the last CES, they'll never forgive us." This time it worked just fine and even garnered light applause.

Bastiaens made an emotional public play to pacify Pachikov by introducing him to the journalists as a Russian who is "more popular than Boris Yeltsin." He invited him onstage and praised his pivotal work. Pachikov admitted that he had not used a Newton to that point, and began by writing, "From Russia with love." The recognizers developed the scrawl one word at a time and translated it as, "From Russia with core." He then wrote a phrase that was oracular in tone: "I never forget this day." Pachikov was prone to speaking in absolutes.

Journalists seemed bored when it came time to hear about Personal Computer Memory Card International Association (PCMCIA) cards, the new, standard credit-card-sized units that would replace mechanically operated disks by storing information and software accessories for Newton and other machines. **Capps liked to say that PCMCIA stood for "Post Code Modulation Central Intelligence Agency" until Joseph Ansenelli, a twenty-three-year-old marketing team member, told him he thought it actually stood for "People Can't Memorize Computer Industry Acronyms."** Capps was amused by Ansenelli's joke, but found his youth disconcerting. "You want to hear something really depressing?" Capps once asked a group of Newton veterans. "Joey was still in high school when we started this project." Ansenelli's response: "Hey, I was a senior."

Nearly five-and-a-half years into the project, everyone was feeling drained. Morale was low, and back in Cupertino things had deteriorated to the point of petty bickering, as Newton's software engineers accused hardware specialists of eating the entire staff's supply of Reese's peanut-butter cups. Even the press at CES was tired. Where a year earlier they were clamoring to get a good look at Newton, many were now leaving the hotel ballroom before the question-and-answer period—despite the promise of an open bar following the event. O'Mahony surveyed the emptying room at the end of the press conference and noted, "It's a bit disappointing. They're not rushing the stage anymore."

A contestant in a new TV game show called *Quest,* arrives by ferry in San Francisco, where he will
compete in a high-tech scavenger hunt by using the Newton to get his clues. April 1993.

0 0 : 3 2

PROGRAMMER Martin Gannholm came from Sweden in 1989 to work for Bill Atkinson on the
HyperCard project. Now the twenty-four-year-old is a seasoned veteran of the round-the-clock
Newton crash program. He says he needs at least six hours of sleep per night—impossible on this
project. He spends all his waking hours working closely with Steve Capps at Capps' home—and has
even taken over one of Capps' back bedrooms. April 1993.

GRAVITY

D-E-F-Y-I-N-G

May - August 1993

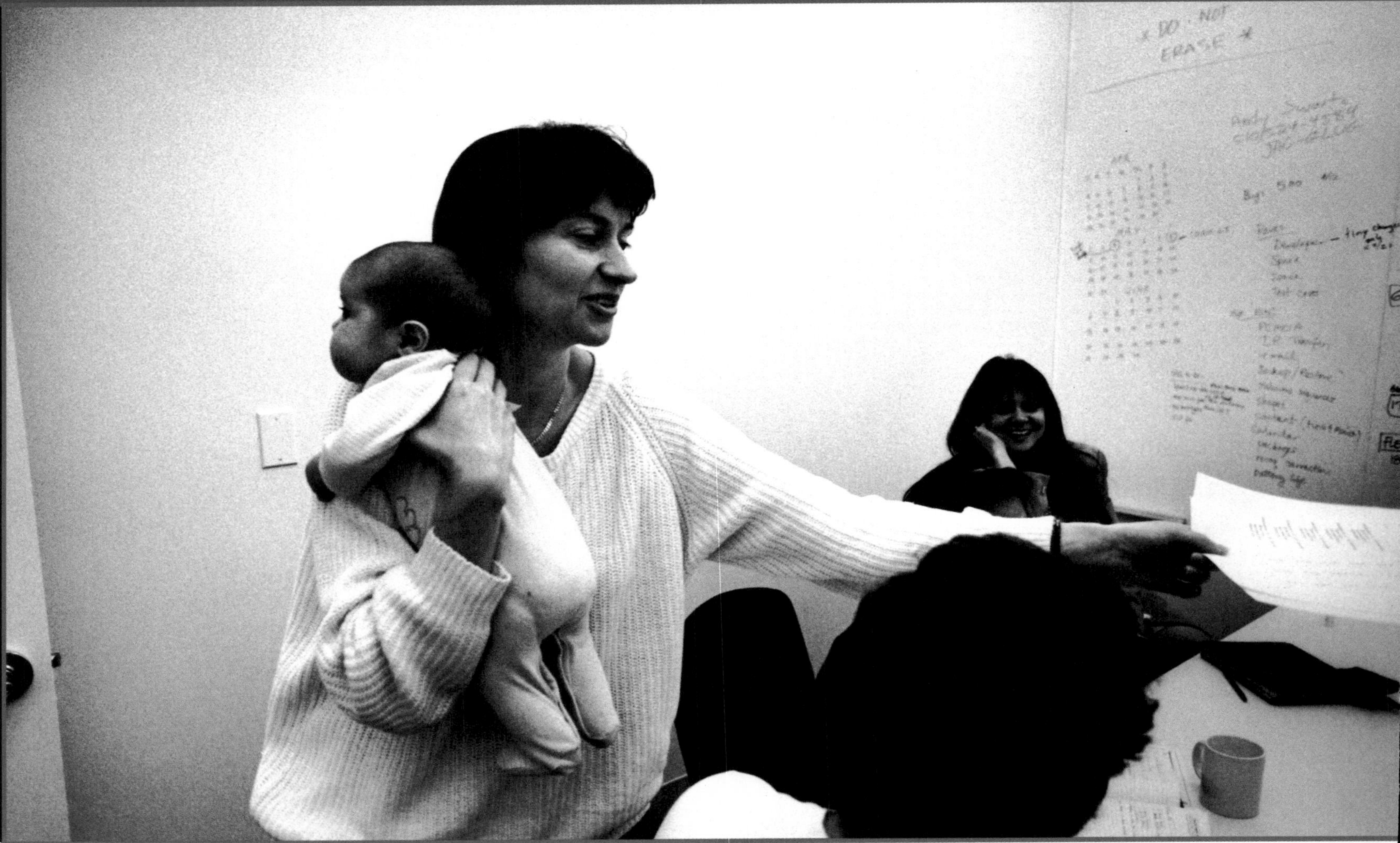

PROGRAMMING engineer Sarah Clark delivers a message to the War Room. Clark often brings her newborn baby to work. She pulls the curtains over the glass walls of her office so colleagues can tell when it's nap time. May 1993.

0 0 : 2 9

June swoon: An affliction that usually affects the San Francisco Giants, causing them to start losing games and any lead they have during the first month of summer. 1993 was different. Thanks to Barry Bonds, the Giants were gaining a lead in their first-place standing. While the swoon seemed to have passed over the San Francisco baseball team, it was hitting the Bay Area further south in Silicon Valley. The entire computer industry was in a serious slump. By mid-month, Apple's stock was in a free-fall, product prices were being slashed, its computers were sold with instant rebates and Sculley announced he was stepping down as CEO while maintaining his position as chairman. The *San Jose Mercury News* bannered the headline: "Sculley reign ends."

Sculley fueled rumors that he would be leaving Apple entirely by telling *USA Today* that he was interested in moving back East and on to the next challenge, once Apple's house was back in order. And, if his own troubles were not bad enough, headlines across the country were reporting that a product he once pushed was possibly tainted. Syringes were being falsely reported in cans of Diet Pepsi, and Sculley watched his friends at PepsiCo flailing as they tried to control the damage.

Apple's inevitable layoffs were just around the corner, and speculation ran that they would be as bad as those in 1985. Now the magic number would be 2,500 deleted jobs, about 15 percent of its 16,000-strong worldwide work force—significantly less than the 35,000 job reductions IBM would announce on July 27th along with its $8 billion loss, but still significant. In the time between Apple's announcement of layoffs and the distribution of pink slips, the only noticeable productivity around the company—outside the PIE division, that is—appeared to be the furious drafting of résumés.

THE day after resigning as CEO, Sculley was in a surprisingly upbeat mood and visited the Newton team where he and Tchao practiced "beaming" information from one Newton to another using Newton's infrared capability. Aside from being somewhat stunned over Sculley's resignation, the team's mood was ebullient since the project was nearly done. June 1993.

basement, unfounded stories abounded of pre-Newton release company buyout attempts by AT&T. Despite a 7 percent revenue increase over the preceding year, in mid-July Apple announced its largest quarterly loss ever, $188.3 million for the third quarter of 1993. Stock options that longtime Apple employees once considered "golden handcuffs" had, for Capps, become more like "balsa-wood handcuffs," financial shackles neither attractive nor strong enough to bind anyone to the company. Spindler, Apple's president and new CEO, was hard at work and out of sight. He issued only optimistic public statements, saying, "We're confident we can put our business back on a growth path by aggressively pursuing market share while offering innovative technology."

As Sculley's former speechwriter, CJ Maupin, now based in Paris, understood Apple, "It's a company that doesn't have a pension plan. It's not a place that you're supposed to come and park for your entire career. We hope that people will come to Apple and give us the best years of their lives, and when they burn out, they can go and start other companies that are also part of the Apple community."

The Bay Area rumor mill was churning hard, particularly on electronic bulletin boards. As Apple's stock slid further down into the NASDAQ bargain

JAMES Joaquin takes a time-out before another meeting in a long day of meetings. Besides working many hours a day getting Newton ready, Joaquin has just taken a lease on a San Francisco storefront where he will open an Extra Large clothing franchise, a company he helped found, and which created the first clothes based on oversized, hip-hop designs. June 1993.

Problems were plaguing all of Apple, and Newton was not exempt. It was not at all clear that the new Golden Master date of June 27th was going to be met. Sculley had staked much of the company's future on the apparently overdue and, some thought, teasingly overpromoted Newton—the first Apple product he could claim as resulting from his own vision and not Jobs' Macintosh work. With the future of the company depending on Sculley's new business plan and its reliance on the perennially delayed MessagePad, the seemingly imperturbable Sculley was feeling the heat. Though he looked confident in public, from June on, Sculley went to bed at night only to "wake up in cold sweats, wondering if there was going to be a product."

While Sculley was having difficulty sleeping, other members of the Newton team were depressed about making product deadlines. Sculley's assistant, Daniel Paul, his eyes and ears in the entertainment industry, occasionally alerted him to morale problems. Paul called his boss and told him, "You need to talk to Michael Tchao, he's kind of down."

Sculley knew that Newton's success depended on the emotional state of its creators, the engineers like Capps and Culbert: "You are dependent entirely on a bunch of artists. If they don't have a good week, you don't have a good week." Corporate management of creative types required managers to deal with them as individuals who were motivated by emotional incentive and understanding. While in other industries, absenteeism could mean slacking on the job, in Capps' case, it meant he was working even harder and more efficiently. It was yet another reminder for Sculley that he was not running a company approximating the PepsiCo school of management, where employee

VIKKI Pachera, standing at whiteboard, leads a meeting in the War Room to review the manufacturing progress, a complex process she manages, made more complex as the software required to build the Newtons slips past deadlines. Paula McDermott helps Vikki track the project. May 1993.

EVERY evening the children of the Newton engineers can be seen roaming the halls of the research lab, playing and visiting with their parents. Here they are helping out by creatively rewriting some technical product specifications and strategy diagrams. May 1993.

MARGE Boots gives programmer Phil Beiser pointers on how to use the rowing machine in the nearby Apple gym. Both work out regularly to combat stress. May 1993.

locking entries in machine
Docker Changes
RAM
CPU
LCD
NO Release

TRICIA Chan is starting another marathon day, this one at the Apple Developer's Conference, where she discusses upcoming demos with other Newton team members. May 1993.

0 0 : 2 3

productivity, success and reward were easily quantifiable in dollars and cents, and by graphing sales, profit and market share.

A subtle change occurred toward the end of June. Things were so lousy at Apple and so many things had gone wrong that it began to seem as if there were nowhere to go but up. A crucial adrenalin spurt appeared, although the finish line was not entirely in sight. Maybe it came from the sense that this was a last-chance challenge that needed to be met at all costs. In any case, there was no particular event or change that seemed to inspire the new aggressiveness and hopefulness that suddenly arose in Sculley and the Newton team members.

A week before Golden Master was scheduled for completion, Sculley took the marketing offensive at the Digital World conference in Los Angeles, deftly confronting criticism and combating misperceptions during a CNN interview. At the end of a day when he delivered a keynote at the conference, he had scheduled a dinner with Annette Bening and Warren Beatty at their home. Sculley had complained earlier to Daniel Paul that no one ever paged him. At dinner, an unexpected beep went off and Sculley pulled out his pager to check it. Beatty told him he had always wanted a beeper, so Sculley handed

00:22

ENGINEERS at Disabled Programmers Inc., known to the Newton team as "Beta Town," watch as Michael Tibbott reads their bug reports. DPI is under contract to Apple to rigorously test the Newton software, and they have been providing invaluable detailed findings on a weekly basis. June 1993.

JOSEPH Ansanelli, 22, was in high school when the Newton project began. Youngest of the very young and very bright marketing group, Ansanelli has been baptized into the religion of new technology during this project. He now has a sign on his door that reads "Forty-eight months till sabbatical," which refers to the two month break granted five-year employees. May 1993.

00:21

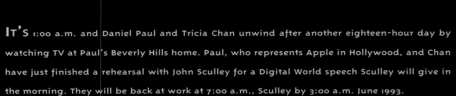

IT'S 1:00 a.m. and Daniel Paul and Tricia Chan unwind after another eighteen-hour day by watching TV at Paul's Beverly Hills home. Paul, who represents Apple in Hollywood, and Chan have just finished a rehearsal with John Sculley for a Digital World speech Sculley will give in the morning. They will be back at work at 7:00 a.m., Sculley by 3:00 a.m. June 1993.

ANXIOUS software developers crowd around James Joaquin, back-to-camera, to get more details about Newton Toolkit, the software that will allow them to write applications for Newton, and to hear about Apple's plans for them. Joaquin has just helped demonstrate the Toolkit at the Apple Developer's Conference in San Jose. Later, Tony Espinoza gave a demo of the Toolkit to the even more cynical MacHack conference. He endured cat calls through most of the presentation. However, the tone eventually changed as hackers were won over by the Toolkit's features and actually began cheering. At the end, the crowd leapt to its feet and gave Newton Toolkit and Espinoza a standing ovation chanting, "Newton, Newton, Newton" May 1993.

00:20

his over for Beatty to see. Sculley then pushed a button so that the actor could read the message Paul had sent: "Don't forget to eat your vegetables." Everyone laughed at the joke.

Despite myriad problems in the topsy-turvy computer business, Newton was beginning to turn into the company's one shining star. News reports were trickling out to the public about Newton as Apple's remaining hope, with many articles pointing out that Apple was one of the few companies in the computer industry willing to risk massive resources—with dollar figures the tightest held secret within the company—in research and development to try to come out with something entirely new. And by now, almost done. Again. Young Ansanelli hooked onto a cliché to describe how he looked ahead and could "see the light at the end of the tunnel. The only problem is I don't know if it's an oncoming train."

The operating software was nearing completion as Culbert went through his twenty-seventh and final hardware build. On Sunday, June 27th, the eighth candidate for Golden Master was sent to Japan so Sharp could burn it into ROM chips that would go into the final manufactured MessagePad. Programming went on nonstop from the lackluster CES at the beginning of the

month until that Sunday at 5:00 p.m. P.S.T.—on time according to the new schedule, but in fact a full year later than Sculley had hoped. All the final bugs that had to be squashed were gone, and the code could now be downloaded to Japan over a modem line—a fifty-minute connection that would be confirmed by a follow-up call to Sharp headquarters. Yes!

Pop went the ceremonial bottle of champagne. A smiling Tesler, no longer an active part of the Newton team, came by with his daughter to show his support for everyone's accomplishments and to enjoy the celebration. Newton's software and hardware teams toasted each other in that moment of relief and subdued fear. **The code was as good as they could get it by this date, but there was always, always, always a chance that there would be a hidden bug that could make the machine malfunction.** Talk of bugs was not the theme, however, as the tired "Branch Newtonians" (as the cloistered group came to be known at Apple following the Branch Davidian episode in Waco) looked back on nearly six years of hard work.

Nine years earlier, before Macintosh was shipped, Jobs had insisted that the employees who worked on the project inscribe and sign their names

full-screen newt that can be made to appear instead of the Newton light bulb logo and a "Find Elvis" feature that accesses a world map and time zone screen stating, "The King was last seen in Paris," or Rome or Tokyo . . . or anywhere else in the world, depending on where Newton Intelligence tracks down Elvis' last sighting.

Sculley, whose excitement was already rekindled, knew that each production delay had made it harder for him to keep the project alive. He reflected on how he worked "to create 'air cover' so that other people wouldn't try to shoot it down." Now that the ROM was done, he was starting to heave a slow, cautious sigh of relief. "We're actually about a year behind the schedule that we had hoped we would be to bring it to market, but the product we're bringing to market is even better than we could have envisioned when we agreed to go ahead with this back in 1990."

The final weeks before the August 2nd launch in Boston were frenzied. Apple sent Newton team members to Japan to check the production line at Sharp, where they were highly restricted from looking at Sharp's version of the Newton and found themselves outnumbered in last-minute discussions over general post-assembly quality control issues. Apple was also trying to

on the inside of each computer's housing. The Newton engineers took a page out of this tradition and installed a credit roll into the ROM, showing screen after screen of the handwritten names of those who constructed the heart and soul of this newest machine. The final screen was dedicated to the memory of Ko Isono.

There were other hidden surprises built into the ROM that will remain hard to access, stuck there for eternity. A love note from Capps to his wife, a

APPLE Manufacturing and Quality Engineer David Pierce, back-to-camera, faces a team of Sharp engineers during an all-day meeting at Sharp's factory in Nara, Japan. Pierce is responsible for Newton quality and is here to work out plans for Newton manufacturing quality control. Product Quality General Manager Kazuyuki Nakano, center, gestures as he responds to Pierce's questions about Sharp reporting procedures. July 1993.

VIKKI Pachera takes a commuter train to the Sharp factory in Nara, Japan, to see the first Newtons come off the assembly line. As one of the key women on the Newton team, Pachera is fond of saying that Scully "set her up for success" when he personally introduced her to Sharp senior executives, and she was given full production responsibility for the MessagePad. July 1993.

SHARP'S Akira Mitarai reviews cue cards for a video interview he is making for Apple's upcoming Newton product launch with Assistant Manager Yasushi Yamamoto and producer Bruce Mac Donell, left, at Sharp's factory in Nara, Japan. July 1993.

DON Louv, whose official title reads "Wild Newt Tamer," walks through the Sharp assembly line while the first Newtons are being built. Louv designed the tests required to prove that the software code Capps and crew wrote actually works as intended. He has come to test a software "patch" that he expects will kill the last bug in the extremely complex Newton software. July 1993.

make sure enough communications features were included in the first product so the company could conduct a marketing campaign aimed at defining Newton as a communications tool with intelligent assistance and divert attention from handwriting recognition technology. Callers dialing 1-800-7-NEWTON heard a hokey, commercial-sounding voice that chided those who expected handwriting recognition to be perfect: "Newton's law number 84: Penmanship declines with every year of education." The rest of the original message on the 800-number did more to attract attention to poor recognition than draw callers to communications features.

While trying to obfuscate certain problems, Newton's marketing and engineering teams concentrated on communications and worked closely with Motorola by inviting its testers to Cupertino to check out the critical pager card in Apple's labs. Though the mechanical part of the pager for which Motorola was responsible was nearly complete, negotiations were still proceeding with a national pager service company. These talks stalled five days before launch, sending Apple scrambling to close a deal with BellSouth.

LESS than two weeks from the Boston launch date of August 2nd, the very first Newtons to be built for sale move down the assembly line where workers complete final assembly at Sharp's Nara, Japan, factory. July 1993.

tional and fundamental programs. The process of developing software for personal computers was long and arduous. The Mac platform required third-party developers to write new software before it could take off. And take off it did, thanks to Macintosh's unique graphics abilities and early domination of the desktop publishing industry through new software and the introduction of the near-typeset quality LaserWriter. **But the Newton development tools would require neither much time nor a high degree of programming sophistication for software authors—just ideas and dedication. And writing for Newton could be done on the Macintosh. Programmers did not need a Newton to write for a Newton.** Apple invited selected third-party developers to come to Cupertino for intense ten-day "adoption" programs, where they learned how to program for the Newton, and then set off to develop the applications that could prove critical to Newton's acceptance in the marketplace. The Newton team demanded that developers make entire completed software packages or games in a matter of a couple of months—a development period unheard of in traditional software publishing.

There was also a push to get as many software titles as possible published before Newton hit the stores. Although development tools were not complete until a couple of months before the launch, the Newton team felt it had to have at least a couple of dozen third-party PCMCIA-packed programs and games for the Newton platform to be taken seriously by industry analysts. When the Macintosh was introduced over a decade earlier, it was bundled with only two software packages, MacWrite and MacPaint, both func-

RAY Riley watches while Scott Petry takes sandpaper to the rough edge of a Newton he just sawed down to fit in a display case. They were preparing a selection of prototypes for future Newton products to be shown the next morning at the Newton launch. August 1993.

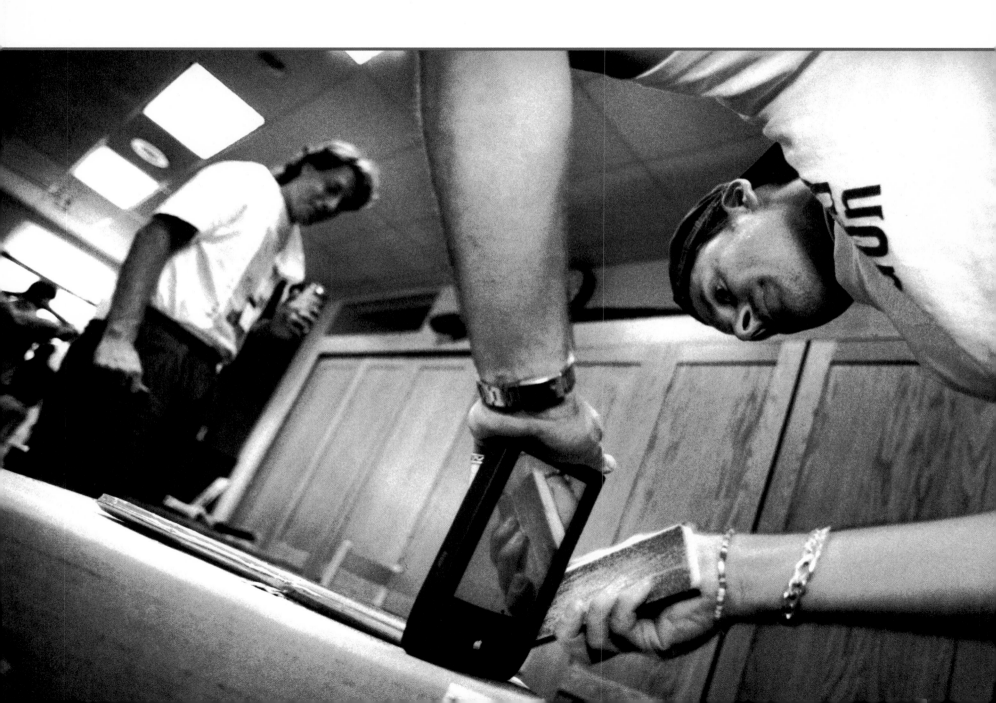

DURING a rehearsal for the Newton launch, Christopher Escher, head of Apple's corporate public relations, advises Michael Tchao and others on stage to look directly at the audience. August 1993.

Everything was coming down to the last minute, including the packaging of the final product. Just a few weeks before the launch, Newton engineers were told they might have to pack boxes of MessagePads in their hotel rooms in Boston so they could have enough for sale in the few retail chains carrying the product. Vikki Pachera nixed that idea when she saw a programming genius clumsily drop a Newton he was casually holding. So, instead, the packaging went to an Apple warehouse in Sacramento and was sent to Boston by air courier.

Unfortunately for Pachera, units that came off the assembly line in Japan were flawed. The little rubber tips that went on the bottom of the MessagePad were falling off the product, so she and a few others drove to California's capital city and spent an entire day gluing 800 of the no-slip grips that Newton team members affectionately called "nipples."

That was not all. The PCMCIA card that was enclosed in each Newton package, including a "Getting Started" guided tour of the device and a word game, failed to work. Pop in the PCMCIA and . . . nothing. Apple at first suspected that Sharp caused the problem during manufacturing, but troubleshooting showed that the fault was in software written at Apple. Software "patches" had to be written so the code could be circumvented. The patch would hide the problem in the extant software. Once it was written, it had to be applied by hand. Two thousand PCMCIA cards were inserted into MessagePads for patching before they were packed in boxes and shipped.

None of these last-minute problems and changes seemed to affect the general upbeat mood of the Newton teams. It all seemed relatively minor in the grand scheme of things. In fact, problems were to be expected. They seemed natural. But they were certainly insignificant compared to the natural disaster in late July that caused flooding in the Midwest, which provided a surreal backdrop for the national introduction of the Newton MessagePad's abilities.

On Friday, July 30th, *Good Morning America's* weather reporter Spencer Christian was on the scene of a flooded riverbank in Des Moines with water rushing behind him as he gave a dramatic report of the devastation. Meanwhile, back on the set in New York, Michael Tchao was on the phone behind the stage, a few feet away from Sculley. "Dad?" he whispered.

The man on the other end of the phone in Maine answered the early morning call. "Michael?"

"Dad, turn to Channel 8, 'cause I'm going to be on *Good Morning America* in five minutes." The producer was looking to get Tchao onstage for the broadcast when Tchao's mother got on the phone. "Michael? How's the house? Are you redecorating?"

"I have to get off the phone now, Mom." Tchao returned to the stage to take his place next to Sculley, in time for them to perform a flawless demonstration of Newton technology and the final MessagePad product. **They both had been worried that the demonstration had to be done live and were particularly concerned that they had been asked to fax to a machine next to Christian in a part of the country where phone lines were continually failing.** In fact, throughout rehearsal for the program, all attempts to get the phone lines up and working to Des Moines had failed. Until it came time for the real thing, that is, when Christian gave the thumbs up, yanked the paper coming out of the fax machine and waved the faxed message—making it hard to read—in front of the camera, showing a national audience that, indeed, Newton worked! It was an Apple coup and made for such great live television that the producers at NBC's *Today Show* complained because they were not offered the first chance to host Sculley and test Newton.

Afterwards, Sculley told Tchao that "there were fifteen million viewers watching, and more people just saw you than have ever seen you before in your life." Sculley expected a snappy retort from Tchao since "he's always got a great comeback, but for the first time since I've known him, he was speechless." Tchao's silence probably had less to do with his own TV appearance than it did with MessagePad's. The gadget he had fought so hard to get produced had just spoken more eloquently than anything he could say; after all, Tchao's life had revolved entirely around the development of this product. And now Newton had a life of its own.

Newton was on a roll. **Not only had the MessagePad been demonstrated successfully to a jazzed television team, but most major newspapers in the country had written neutral to favorable pre-launch pieces.** The notable exception was the critically important *Wall Street Journal*, which panned the product. Sculley made sure not to show Tchao the *Journal* piece before they went on air.

Apple's new business plan called for partnering with large, recognized, progressive companies so Apple could leverage its experience and expertise while using the supportive partnership to give the appearance of increasing momentum for the MessagePad. Sculley felt that Newton products also had to concentrate on varied communications capabilities to succeed, so Apple pursued both collaborative and exploratory relationships with three Regional Bell Operating Companies, Ameritech, US West and BellSouth.

A look at the Apple-BellSouth relationship:

August 1992 The two companies discuss working together on a "Wizzy Active Lifestyle Telephone" (WALT), an experimental telephone with built-in Newton technology and interface for people who are not computer users. Trials for WALT prototypes are set for early 1993.

Fall 1992 As Apple forms its new PIE division, bureaucratic changes delay development of the prototype and advancement of the relationship.

March 1993 Apple investigates relationships with BellSouth's Yellow Pages group for on-line service possibilities. It also explores possibilities with BellSouth's cellular and paging groups. Parallel talks proceed in wire and wireless communications services and products.

May 1993 BellSouth consolidates and changes some of its divisions in a reorganization of its own. Although WALT prototype units are completed and ready to be tested in home banking through one of BellSouth's customers, Barnet Bank, there are delays. Decision makers' dependence on and trust in personal relationships at both companies are weaknesses during reorganizations when people are being shifted around. BellSouth representatives working with Apple are moved into a new group called BellSouth Technology Services. Apple uses these relationships to find out who the new people in charge are and how to get to them to push along and develop new relationships and old agreements.

June 1993 An announcement is made at CES in Chicago that BellSouth is initiating trials of WALT. BellSouth is concurrently involved in a company-wide review of all contracts, including early Apple agreements. Apple, lucky enough to start with letter "A," is one of the first contracts reviewed and affirmed in time for the CES announcement. The two companies are still pursuing cellular and screen-based telephone relationships, and paging is still being discussed although Apple is already involved in a high-level discussion on paging services with another company.

July 1993 Five days prior to the Newton launch, there is a breakdown in negotiations with another nationwide paging company, which was prepared to provide service to users of Newton's paging card, produced by Motorola. Subra Iyer, who happens to be in Atlanta meeting with BellSouth on an unrelated topic, kicks into gear to start serious negotiations on paging services. After twenty-two straight hours of negotiation, Apple attorney Joe Stockwell finalizes the agreement three days before Newton's launch. Steve Pazian, President at BellSouth, then goes into his study at home so he can be videotaped for a Newton testimonial to be shown on a large screen at Boston Symphony Hall on August 2nd. Pazian observes, "If we had five years to conclude the deal, we still probably wouldn't have closed until the last five days." Newton counsel David Farrington sums it up: "At very big companies, it usually takes a long time to make a decision, but once they've decided, you can move very quickly to finalize."

0 0 :

The day finally arrived for the launch: August 2nd. The place: Boston Symphony Hall. Guests had difficulty getting to the hall since the street was cordoned off for the funeral of Reggie Lewis, the twenty-seven-year-old Boston Celtics player whose unexpected death shocked the country. Inside, the hall was set up with Newton point-of-purchase displays with built-in working devices. In the center of the hall were booths for third-party devel-

opers who brought twenty-five Newton software titles to the floor, titles to which Tom Clancy and Tom Selleck had given the celebrity nod that morning.

The night before, Capps stayed up until 2:00 a.m. working on fake applications to run on "show car" models of futuristic Newton prototypes—HyperCard stacked applications, for example, that showed how an aviation company might use Newton to maintain its aircraft. Not only was Capps hacking and checking these fake applications, but he was also adding small artistic flourishes and inside jokes that no one was ever likely to notice.

Everything moved quickly the morning of August 2nd. Sculley understood the phenomenon viscerally, but had difficulty explaining how things fell into place in the end: "On these real breakthrough products, it always seems to come together in the last four days." It was magic. The day before the launch was devoted to rehearsing speeches and product demonstrations. Engineers and managers from different Apple divisions were getting their first glimpse of the MessagePad and were being taught by a media specialist how to demonstrate them and how to handle questions from the press—"Never, ever give out any numbers—like the number of engineers working on Newton—and never go 'off the record' with information."

FROM left, Gaston Bastiaens, John Sculley and Subra Iyer host a meeting with Matsushita executives from Panasonic, Assistant General Manager William Gardner, Executive Vice President Akira Fujio, and Panasonic Project Manager, Yasuhiko Isobe, at far right taking pictures. Matsushita has licensed Newton technology and plans to produce products through its Panasonic subsidiary. Although the meeting was held minutes before the crucial 10:00 a.m. Newton launch, the Apple executives took their time, had coffee with their guests and acted completely at ease. August 1993.

DONNA Auguste gestures to the crowd after the entire Newton team has taken a bow on stage at Boston Symphony Hall at the end of the launch event. Auguste worked with a speech coach to overcome her stage fright. August 1993.

0 5

The product was complete. There was nothing to do but introduce it and let those who used it judge for themselves. The event producers threw together a hyped, convoluted video and stage production using a Paul Revere "revolutionary" theme—"Newton is coming! Newton is coming!"—but attendees were tired of the seemingly endless talk about what Newton was and would do. They wanted to see for themselves. The flawed onstage demonstrations and the loud music, strobe lights and puffery were fleeting, the speeches forgotten moments after they were uttered.

Suddenly, the product that had taken so long to develop and launch was on autopilot and was bigger than all that surrounded it. Momentum carried it and the gravity of business problems and technical challenges no longer kept it down. Newton was no longer coming. Newton was here.

. . . . .

Cabs were racing all over Boston, swirling around rotaries as they headed to the airport to pick up those arriving for the Macworld conference. Atop their roofs were advertisements with pictures of MessagePads and three simple words: "Now Taking Orders."

Tchao, Capps, Culbert and Sculley, wearing shorts, were strolling down the sunny side of boutique-lined Newbury Street two days before Newton's launch, with the occasional passer-by stopping to look at Sculley—the corporate celebrity who graced magazine covers and received serious TV exposure when he sat next to Hillary Rodham Clinton during the President's first State of the Union address. Just before their walk to lunch, Capps and Culbert were in Tchao's hotel suite at the Four Seasons, where Capps saw a picture in a magazine of a tiny, palm-sized, pen-based product concept. "That's the size Newton I want to make," said Capps. He turned to Culbert. "Hey, Mike, can you make something this small?"

Culbert took a look and, without hesitating, said, "Yeah, sure, no problem," and suggested a possible processor for the device.

Capps' wheels were turning as the four now headed toward lunch. He posed his idea to Sculley.

"John, how about something the size of your pager with a card file in it and ink notes?"

Sculley pulled out his SkyTel pager from his clip-on belt holster as if he were drawing a gun in a showdown at high noon. Capps pulled out his, too, as they marched down the street. Sculley pointed at the limited line mini-

0 0 : 0 3

GASTON Bastiaens shares a toast to Newton's success with Tom Clancy, middle, and Tom Selleck an hour after the Boston introduction of Newton at the Boston Symphony Hall. Clancy and Selleck attended the launch because they are interested in how Newtons could help with their work with the Kyle Foundation, which aids seriously ill children. August 1993.

AN elated group of Newton veterans gathered with John Sculley to pose for the media on stage just after the successful and long-awaited Newton introduction at Boston Symphony Hall. August 1993.

ENGINEER Maurice Sharp does the limbo at the party celebrating Newton's product introduction earlier in the day. By midnight, it's clear these engineers intend to try to balance out in this one evening their six years of intense effort with equally intense partying. August 1993.

screen on the alphanumeric pager and asked, "What kind of functionality would it have?"

Tchao, picking up on Sculley's interest, jumped into the discussion. "Infrared and one-way paging."

Sculley was looking for more: "If you had two-way paging . . . ." Then everyone hopped into the idea-generation mill. Culbert talked about costs and possible hardware processors, while Capps, the master at user interface, was already figuring out how to make the information easily accessible. Sculley then pointed out that a quick hack of this technology could create a clear competitive advantage to fit his larger business model. "That's the way to knock Gates out: Paging. He's still trying to figure out how to connect to computers."

Cost had to be kept down, too, so Tchao was discouraging some of the added functionality because "two-way paging gets it to over $300."

The first Newton product was barely on store shelves and the core team was already brainstorming about the future. There was a general realization that Sculley's influence had diminished since the days of the flight to Japan that productized Newton; as Apple's chief visionary emeritus and ambassador to the world at large, his functions now were more ceremonial than substantive. He was providing "the vision thing" for Spindler, who was playing Waldo with the press and refusing publicly to say "boo" about anything to anyone outside the corporate boardroom. Sculley was in semi-retirement, planning a sabbatical, when he would be sailing the new boat he was building.

Capps asked the critical question about finding support for the project: "How do we get Gaston?"

Sculley offered his lobbying efforts and mentioned that he was planning to meet Bastiaens for dinner that night. He was worried that Newton would now be just one part of a dissipated marketing and product development effort, with more of Apple's diminishing resources going to the PowerPC, a new line of personal computers planned for 1994. The question, one that hangs in the air with every change in movie studio head or creative company boss, was whether a change of leadership would mean a radical change of direction. In Hollywood, projects in development tended to die on the vine because they were championed by the previous leader; with industries in the Silicon Valley converging with those of the San Fernando Valley, it was unclear if the ethic and practices of the two would also approximate each other.

His Newton vision now complete, Sculley was concerned about implementing his long-term business plan and keeping Newton alive with both the board and Spindler: "You don't have to do eleven things at once. You just have to do one thing right. I'm trying to get Michael behind it. As soon as it becomes successful, he'll be behind it. It is not well understood among the management of the company."

Sculley then turned to Tchao, Culbert and Capps—all still excited about their new, Newton technology-based product brainstorming—as they headed for a patio table at American Joe's Bar and Grill. In the simplest way possible, he defined the only strategy he saw for the beleaguered Apple to survive at the end of the Sculley era: "Focus on Newton."

AFTER six years of struggle—personal and professional—the Newtonians exult in a Boston nightclub. They were a small team faced with a prodigious task but, in the end their goals were achieved: a new technology for a new market and a new business model for Apple. They party, like many nights before, gyrating toward first light. August 1993.

Thank You:

Rene Adomshick Ann Almeida John Altberg Kirk Anspach Efi Arazi Stephanie Arvisu Michelle August Donna Auguste Anette Ayala Gaston Bastiaens Mark Bauman

Jeff Baxter Karen Bellantoni Bob Bengtson Richard Bernstein Susanne Biedenkopf Cindy Black Hannah Bloch Gene Blumberg, CPA Chrissy Boggs Marge Boots Larry

Boxer Randy Bradley Heidi Bradner Russell Brown Scott Brownstein Adam Budish Robert Burns Gary, Joann and Andy Cameron Steve Capps Carnahan, Smith and

Gunter Mike and Gina Cerre Tricia Chan David, Devyani, Kara and Willie Cohen

Richard Cohn Eleanor Craig Michael Crichton Judith Crist Burt Cummings Kathy

Dalle-Molle Marie D'Amico Pietro Del Re Ray and Barbara DeMoulin Mark

Doolittle Andy Dreyfus Dynagraphics earwax productions Dr. Charles A. Eck

Owen Edwards Claudia Encinas Elliott Erwitt Jennifer Erwitt Christopher Escher

Exact Imaging eyejam productions Dan Farber David Farrington Philip Feldman

Diane Festa Joan Finkle Nick Gage Martin Gannholm Lavander Ginsberg Tom

Ginsberg Bill Gladstone and family Avra Gordis Marshal Greene Pauline

Hageman Acey Harper and family Tim Harrington Rick Hawley Sam Hoffman Rafi Holtzman Peter Howe Doedy Hunter James Joaquin Barney Jones Bill and Sara Joy

Susan Kare Guy Kawasaki Douglas and Francoise Kirkland Josef Klima Alex Knight Susan Koe Petr and Hana Konvalinkovi Todd Koons Antonios and Vasiliki

Kounalakis Diane Kounalakis Barbara Krause Philip Krohn Eliane Laffont Jean Pierre Laffont Peter Laufer Jean Francois Leroy Lincoln and Allen Charlotte and

Byron Liske Julie Livingston Arsenio Lopez Betulia Machado Jackson Machado Maria Tereza Machado Mary Magill Nina Maksudova Margot Maley Justine Marquit CJ Maupin Steve Mays Georgia McCabe Michael McDowell Jim McKee D. Barry Menuez Paolo Menuez Rona Michele Phillip Moffitt and Cheryl MacLachan Clement Mok James Molesky Marvin Moore Debbie Morris Karen Mullarkey Andy Murdoch Rachel Myers Matthew Naythons Karen Nazor Duane

Nelson Linda Stone Neumann Marco Nicoletti Gerri Nietzel Rod Nordland Bob Oliver Jon Olsen Frank O'Mahony Fran, Catherine and Michael Ortiz Vikki Pachera Tim Parsey Roger Patton Daniel Paul Scott Petry Terry Phillips Principia Graphica Gina Privitere Patti Richards Robin and Heidi Rickabaugh Tom Rielly Ray Riley Denise Rocco Joan Rosenberg Michael Rothbard Paul Saffo Arthur Sainer Steve Salzman Pamela Sansbury Peter Sartorius Karen Schein Barry Schiffman Rochelle Schiffman Gabi Schindler Brent Schlender Susan Schuman Tom Scott John Sculley Nina Sederholm Anna, Nico and Juan Sever Donald Shanor Steve Sherman and Family Bruce Shostak Karen Sipprell Walter Smith Rick Smolan Don Snyder David and Cissy Spindler Ellen Spooren Mrs. Harley C. Stevens Marisha Swart Jay Tannenbaum Michael Tchao Larry Tesler Brad and Julie Topliff Mary Jane Treloar Hajime Ueda Carole Underwood Della van Heyst Jean and Alan Venable Thomas K. Walker Josh Weisberg Karen Wickre Michael Witlin Susan Woodrum Keith Yamashita Marla Zanatto Eric Zarakov

SPECIAL THANKS TO THE FOLLOWING COMPANIES FOR THEIR SUPPORT

3M Company

AGFA Division, Miles, Inc.

Electronics for Imaging, Inc.

Gilbert Paper

Graphics Resource

Ilford Photo Corporation

Spindler Photographics Services

SUPERMAC Technologies, Inc.

TechArt

THE LAND AND THE PEOPLE: *The Republic of China*
Photographer: Tim Harmon; Introduction: Madame Chiang Kai-shek • 144 pages, 114 color and five black-and-white photos, 11 x 11 inches, $39.95 hardbound

The photographer was granted permission to journey to areas of Taiwan formerly restricted to foreigners. His sensitive images capture the feelings of the land, its people in both work and play and the spirit that inspires this country. Included are groundbreaking photos that glimpse into the lives of seven aboriginal tribes living as they have for the past 10,000 years. Accompanying the photos is an entertaining and informative text.

A CIRCLE OF NATIONS: *Voices and Visions of American Indians*
Editor: John Gattuso; Introduction: Michael Dorris; Foreword: Leslie Marmon Silko • 128 pages, 80 color and duotone photographs, 9.5 x 11 inches, $39.95 hardbound

A reflection of the lives of contemporary American Indians, viewed from the Native perspective through essays and writings by well-known American Indian writers and photographers including Paula Gunn Allen, Leslie Marmon Silko, Joy Harjo, Simon Ortiz, White Deer of Autumn, David Neel, Monty Roessel, and Ken Blackbird. Humanity, mystery, change and continuity are the themes of this book. It honors tradition and universal bonds while celebrating diversity and the full range of Native life: family, community, the arts, religion, powwows, politics and other social issues.

LIGHT ON THE LAND: *A World Landscape Book*
Photographer: Art Wolfe; Author: Art Davidson • 196 pages, 100 color photographs, 14.5 x 11 inches, $75 hardbound

A stunning collection of award-winning landscape photography celebrating the beauty and majesty of the Earth's wilderness, including landscapes from all seven continents. The element of light and the universal theme of "one planet, one light source" is the connecting thread throughout the book. The text is composed of essays and native writings on light and its many aspects: spiritual, biological and physical.

These and other award-winning books are available from the Publisher. All editions are available with customized bound-in pages for gift giving. Write for more information or for our catalogue or quantity-discount schedule, Beyond Words Publishing, Inc., 13950 NW Pumpkin Ridge Road, Hillsboro, Oregon 97124, or call (503) 647-5109.

For more information about the Newton:

NEWTON'S LAW: *The Digital Nomad's Guide to the Newton™ PDA*
Authors: Andrew Gore and Mitch Ratcliffe

Newton's Law is the most authoritative book on the exciting new portable computing/telecommunications device from Apple and Sharp. It has been written by the highly entertaining Andrew Gore and Mitch Ratcliffe, the most knowledgeable mobile computing experts around. Packed with how-to's and troubleshooting tips, this informative guide is based on Gore and Ratcliffe's hard use of the Newton on the road, as well as in-depth interviews with Newton engineers—the guys who actually designed and built the Newton PDA. 224 pages, 7.5 x 9.25 inches, ISBN: 0-679-74647-1, $20 paperback (plus $4.95 shipping and handling) Order from Random House Electronic Publishing, P.O. Box 663, Holmes, PA 19043, or call 1-800-345-8112.

Defying Gravity is also available on CD Rom and audio cassette. Contact Beyond Words Publishing, Inc. for information.